MW00332852

12 Spoons 2 Bowls and a Knife

15 Step-by-Step, Handcarved Projects for the Kitchen

FOX CHAPEL
PUBLISHING

A *Woodcarving Illustrated* Book
www.WoodcarvingIllustrated.com

© 2020 by Fox Chapel Publishing Company, Inc., 903 Square Street, Mount Joy, PA 17552.

12 Spoons, 2 Bowls, and a Knife is an original work, first published in 2020 by Fox Chapel Publishing Company, Inc. The patterns contained herein are copyrighted. Readers may make copies of these patterns for personal use. The patterns themselves, however, are not to be duplicated for resale or distribution under any circumstances. Any such copying is a violation of copyright law.

ISBN 978-1-4971-0114-2

Library of Congress Control Number: 2020938353

To learn more about the other great books from Fox Chapel Publishing, or to find a retailer near you, call toll-free 800-457-9112 or visit us at *www.FoxChapelPublishing.com*.

We are always looking for talented authors. To submit an idea, please send a brief inquiry to acquisitions@foxchapelpublishing.com.

Printed in China
First printing

Because working with wood and other materials inherently includes the risk of injury and damage, this book cannot guarantee that creating the projects in this book is safe for everyone. For this reason, this book is sold without warranties or guarantees of any kind, expressed or implied, and the publisher and the author disclaim any liability for any injuries, losses, or damages caused in any way by the content of this book or the reader's use of the tools needed to complete the projects presented here. The publisher and the author urge all readers to thoroughly review each project and to understand the use of all tools before beginning any project.

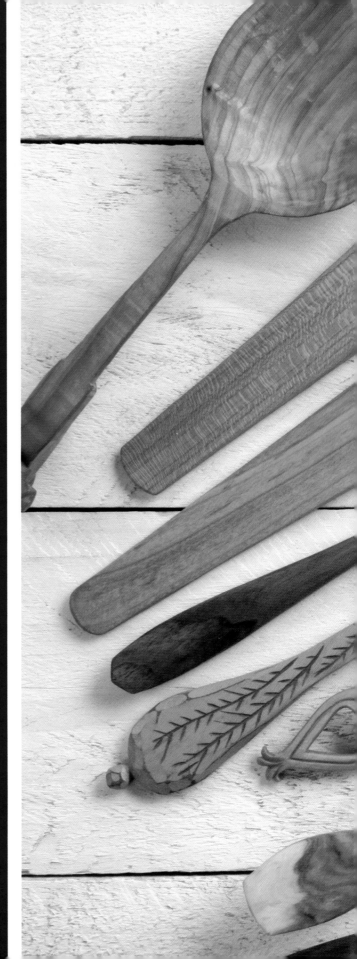

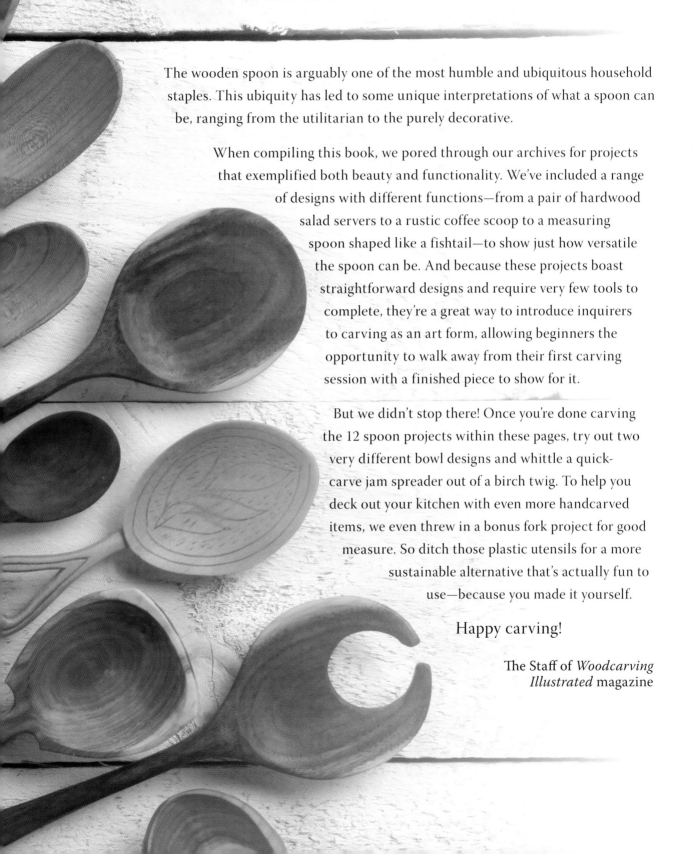

Introduction

The wooden spoon is arguably one of the most humble and ubiquitous household staples. This ubiquity has led to some unique interpretations of what a spoon can be, ranging from the utilitarian to the purely decorative.

When compiling this book, we pored through our archives for projects that exemplified both beauty and functionality. We've included a range of designs with different functions—from a pair of hardwood salad servers to a rustic coffee scoop to a measuring spoon shaped like a fishtail—to show just how versatile the spoon can be. And because these projects boast straightforward designs and require very few tools to complete, they're a great way to introduce inquirers to carving as an art form, allowing beginners the opportunity to walk away from their first carving session with a finished piece to show for it.

But we didn't stop there! Once you're done carving the 12 spoon projects within these pages, try out two very different bowl designs and whittle a quick-carve jam spreader out of a birch twig. To help you deck out your kitchen with even more handcarved items, we even threw in a bonus fork project for good measure. So ditch those plastic utensils for a more sustainable alternative that's actually fun to use—because you made it yourself.

Happy carving!

The Staff of *Woodcarving Illustrated* magazine

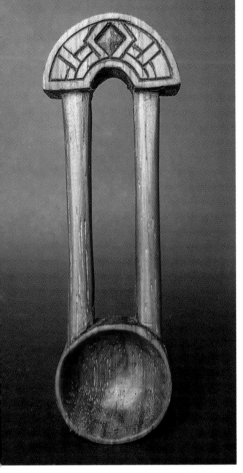

Contents

PROJECTS

Common Spoon Carving Tools

Although always popular, spoon carving is enjoying a renaissance through an influx of carving enthusiasts—young and old alike. Because many new carvers choose spoon carving among their first projects, we thought we'd introduce some tools to make your efforts more enjoyable and successful.

Carving Axe
Carving axes are small, compact, lightweight hatchets perfect for roughly shaping spoon blanks from hewn wood.

Sloyd Knife
Use the large blade on a sloyd-style knife for everything from roughing out to cleaning up the profile and adding details.

Hook Knife
Use a hook knife to hollow and smooth spoon bowls in just a few passes.

Drawknife
Use a drawknife to shave down wood blanks and spoon handles in a balanced way and refine surfaces for future detail work.

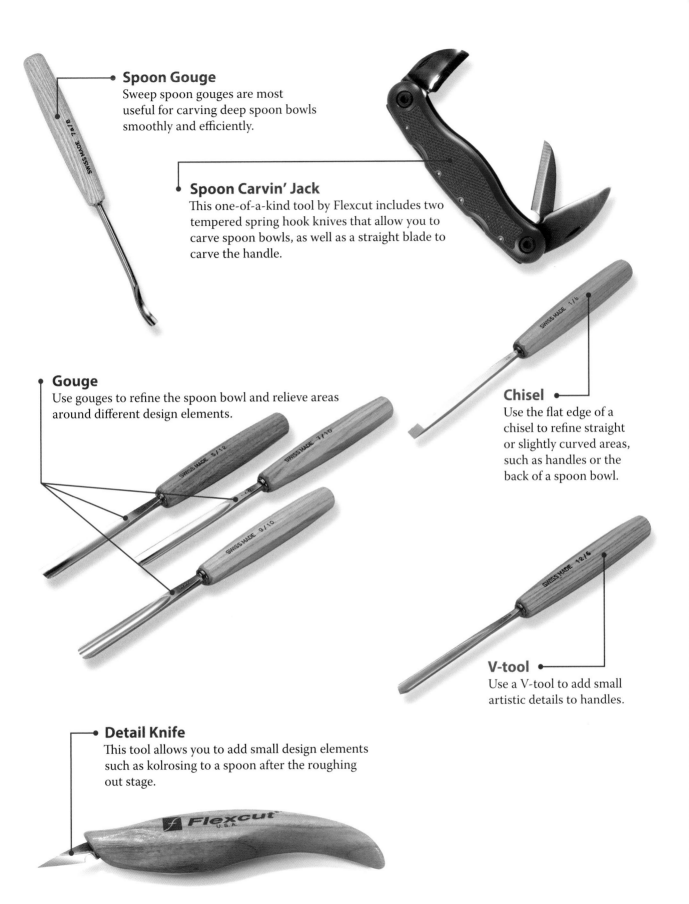

Spoon Gouge
Sweep spoon gouges are most useful for carving deep spoon bowls smoothly and efficiently.

Spoon Carvin' Jack
This one-of-a-kind tool by Flexcut includes two tempered spring hook knives that allow you to carve spoon bowls, as well as a straight blade to carve the handle.

Gouge
Use gouges to refine the spoon bowl and relieve areas around different design elements.

Chisel
Use the flat edge of a chisel to refine straight or slightly curved areas, such as handles or the back of a spoon bowl.

V-tool
Use a V-tool to add small artistic details to handles.

Detail Knife
This tool allows you to add small design elements such as kolrosing to a spoon after the roughing out stage.

Basic Cuts

Like most types of carving (woodcarving, ice carving, stone carving), spoon carving is a subtractive art—you remove all of the material that isn't part of your vision for the final piece. For example, to carve a measuring spoon, remove all of the wood that doesn't contribute to the shape of the measuring spoon.

Most carvers use four basic cuts to remove excess wood: the push cut, the paring cut, the stop cut, and the V-shaped cut. Master these four basic types of cuts and you'll be ready to tackle a multitude of projects.

Stop Cut

As the name suggests, the stop cut is used to create a hard line at the end of another cut. Your hand position depends on the placement of the cut you need to make. Regardless of your hand position, simply cut straight into the wood to create a stop cut. Make a stop cut first to prevent a consecutive cut from extending beyond the intended area. Make a stop cut second to free a chip of wood remaining from a primary cut.

Push Cut

For the push cut, hold the wood in one hand. Hold the knife in your other hand with the thumb on the back of the blade. Push the knife through the wood, away from your body. This type of cut is also called the straightaway cut. For additional control or power, place the thumb of the wood-holding hand on top of the thumb on the blade, and use the wood-holding thumb as a pivot as you rotate the wrist of your knife-holding hand. This maneuver is often called the thumb-pushing cut or lever cut.

Paring Cut

The paring cut gives you a great deal of control but requires you to cut toward your thumb. Wear a thumb protector or be aware of the knife position at all times, especially if it slips beyond the anticipated stopping point. To perform the paring cut, which is also called a draw cut, hold the wood in one hand. Hold the knife in the other hand with four fingers. The cutting edge points toward your thumb. Rest the thumb of your knife-holding hand on the wood behind the area you want to carve. Extend the thumb as much as possible. Close your hand, pulling the knife toward your thumb, to slice through the wood. This is the same action used to peel (or pare) potatoes.

V-Shaped Cut

To make a V-shaped cut, hold a knife the same way you do when making a paring cut. Anchor the thumb of the knife hand against the wood and cut in at an angle with the tip of the knife. Rotate the wood, anchor your thumb on the other side of the cut, and cut in at an angle, running beside the first cut. Angle the two cuts so the bottom or deepest part of each cut meets in the center. This creates a V-shaped groove. Use the center of the cutting edge to make intersecting angled cuts on the corner of a blank, creating V-shaped notches.

Carving Safety

There is risk involved whenever you handle sharp tools. A knife sharp enough to cut through wood will easily cut skin. Most cuts are small nicks that heal quickly and don't leave a scar. However, it's best to follow simple safety procedures to prevent serious injuries.

The fundamental rule when it comes to spoon carving is to be aware not only of where the blade is, but where the blade could go. Wood can change density at any point, and you need to change the amount of pressure you apply on the knife based on the wood density. Imagine pushing hard to cut through a hard knot only to find a softer section of wood behind the knot. The sharp edge will quickly slice through the softer area and cut into whatever is on the other side. The knife doesn't care if it's open air, a carving bench, or your hand.

Boy Scouts are taught to always cut away from themselves. While this is good advice, there are times when you cut toward your thumb, such as when making a paring cut (see page 8). When making a paring cut, wear a leather thumb protector, wrap your thumb with cloth tape, or position your thumb far enough down on the project so if the knife slips, it won't hit your thumb.

Because most cuts occur on the hand holding the project, carvers often wear a cut-resistant glove on that hand. It is possible to prevent cuts by being aware of where the sharp edge can (and probably will) go. Always cut away from yourself when you are removing bark or large amounts of wood. When you are carving finer details, anchor your holding hand to the carving hand. Place the thumb of your holding hand on the back of the thumb on the knife-holding hand when doing a push cut. Alternatively, rest the fingers of your knife hand on the fingers of your holding hand. Anchoring your hands adds stability and control, making it less likely that the knife will slip.

Some spoon carvers use their thighs as carving benches. A cut on your thigh can be serious. Carving on a workbench or table is recommended. If you cut toward your thigh, invest in a strip of leather to protect your leg.

Without proper precautions, a slip of the knife can result in a visit to the emergency room. Follow the above safety rules and you'll never require anything more than a Band-Aid.

Wear a glove on the hand holding your carving.

Wear a thumb guard when cutting toward your thumb.

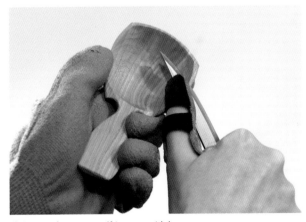
Cut away from yourself to prevent injury.

PROJECTS
FOR EATING

Simple Pocket Spoon

Emmet Van Driesche
Step-by-step photos by Matt White

Pattern on page 88

Small, simple, and mighty are three words that best describe a pocket spoon. Its low profile and strong design make for easy storage and transport. This trade-off is achieved by the lack of a neck; unlike traditional spoon designs, the handle of my pocket spoon is the full width of the bowl. This particular design is fairly simple to try, and also provides a broad canvas for more decorative touches such as chip carving, painting, or kolrosing. *Note: Always wear a carving glove and thumb guard. The photos were taken without them to clearly show hand and knife positions.*

Getting Started

To carve the pocket spoon, I use an axe, a small pruning saw, a straight knife with a large blade, and a hook knife. Use whichever process you're comfortable with. There is no single right way to do this—only whatever works for you and is safe. I also use large, greenwood blanks that have seasoned in the log for several months. This is a very forgiving form, however, and you can achieve great results with many wood types that would prove tricky with other spoon shapes. Use what you have on hand.

Materials & Tools

MATERIALS
- Wood, preferably green and free of knots, 2" (5.1cm) thick: approximately 1½" x 8" (3.8cm x 20.3cm)
- Pencil
- Burnishing items, such as a pebble, bone, antler, or pestle
- Food-safe finish, such as a mixture of beeswax and jojoba oil
- Cotton cloths

TOOLS
- Carving axe or hatchet
- Pruning saw
- Sloyd knife, such as Mora 106
- Hook knife, such as Mora 164

The author used these products for the project. Substitute your choice of brands, tools, and materials as desired.

Special Sources

Emmet used a sloyd knife and hook knife forged by Matt White of Temple Mountain Woodcraft, *templemtnwoodcraft.com*.

PREPARING THE BLANK

Establish the basic shape. With an axe, cut a shallow V into what will be the spoon's top face. This cut establishes the slight difference in angle between the bowl rim and handle, and also sets up the grain flow within the spoon to make it simple to carve.

Draw the spoon shape on the shallow V. You want the bowl of the spoon to straddle the bottom of the V so that ¾" (1.9cm) is on the bowl side and ¼" (0.6cm) is on the handle end. I find it helpful to draw the bowl first, bisect the entire blank with a vertical line, and then use that as the centerline of the handle to help me achieve symmetry.

Cut the perimeter. I used a pruning saw to hack off the ends and removed excess wood from the back and sides with the axe; however, you can use a band saw, if desired. Remember, the axe can cause injuries when used incorrectly, so make sure your pace is slow and careful.

Refine the outline. Use a knife, making sure to keep this cut at a 90° angle to the top face.

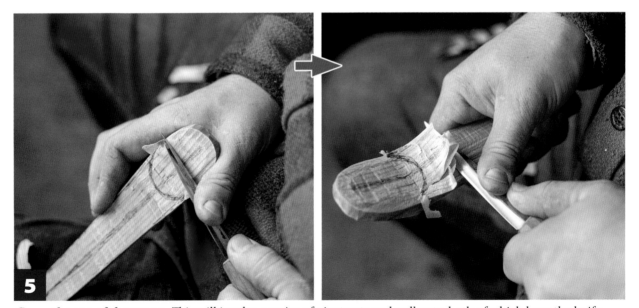

Carve the top of the spoon. This will involve a series of pivot cuts and pull cuts, both of which have the knife facing into my body (read more in the sidebar on page 14). Round the outer edge first, and then thin the neck area down slightly from the top where it begins to dip into the bowl. Ignore the center of the bowl—that will come later.

TIP | ABOUT WOOD MOISTURE

Depending on the level of moisture in the wood, you can either facilitate its release by letting it dry a day or two before finishing, or preserve the moisture by wrapping the spoon in a plastic bag and returning to it later. I prefer wood that has been aged in the log for several months; this tends to have a lower moisture content than freshly cut wood, so I bag my work even if I am stepping away for a few minutes.

6

Refine the bottom of the bowl and handle. Try to remove all axe marks with the knife. Note: You won't reach finished dimensions at this stage.

Pivot Cuts and Pull Cuts

For pivot cuts, the force of my arm pushes out away from me, which is translated into the blade pivoting toward me.

I keep pull cuts controlled and safe by pulling my knife elbow in tight to my side, limiting the potential range of the blade should it slip out of the wood.

7

Redraw the shape with a pencil. This is the chance to figure out, within the reality of what you have done so far, what spoon you can still achieve. Sometimes mistakes or unforeseen difficulties with a particular piece of wood require you to change course slightly. Even when everything goes smoothly, this step will lead you to a better final result.

Repeat steps 4–6. Carve the top and then the bottom of the spoon, bringing everything into as much of a final form as you can. Use the knife to make long, clean, decisive cuts along the bottom, curling the bottom of the bowl at the point where the bowl will begin up top. *Note: Notice I have not carved the bowl at all yet. This is because as long as I haven't carved it, I can adjust the overall shape of the spoon as much as I want. As soon as I start to hollow the bowl, however, this locks the spoon into its final shape and limits my ability to adjust should I make a mistake or uncover a flaw in the wood.*

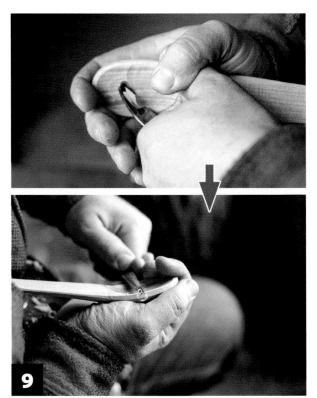

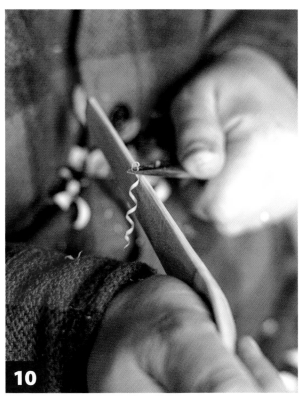

Hollow the bowl. Use a hook knife. I carve spoon bowls the way you'd dig a hole with a shovel: start in the middle and clear out bits of the sides as you go deeper and wider. Once I get the bowl close to where I want it, I take a moment to recut the rim, this time holding the knife flat. Then I finish by carefully establishing the line of the inner rim, and then blending the curvature of the bowl to meet it. Note: Most beginning spoon carvers make bowls too deep, but this one should be kept relatively shallow. Test it out! Put it in your mouth to determine the changes still needed.

Thin down the back of the bowl with the knife. Then make all final cuts, cleaning up areas that appear less smooth and symmetrical than they should be.

Finishing

I always finish my spoons by burnishing them, using either a bit of pebble, bone or antler, or unglazed porcelain (such as a pestle). Burnishing eases down any sharp transitions and blends lines to create a more uniform curve. I then give the piece a quick swipe with a food-safe finish, such as a 2:1 mix of beeswax and jojoba oil, and wipe it clean with a cloth. The spoon is immediately ready to use.

Breakfast Spoon and Fork Set

Elizabeth Sherman

Pattern on page 88

I love working with walnut! The contrast of the dark wood and the green milk paint remind me of my grandmother's kitchen in her home in the mountains. When devising the shape of the spoon and fork set, I imagined using the fork for a small fruit salad and the spoon for serving sides like rice.

I mostly use kiln-dried wood because it's what I have access to. Local woodworkers let me recycle their wood cutoffs, so I have a large supply. While I occasionally carve with green wood, I prefer dried wood for the ease of storage.

Materials & Tools

MATERIALS
- Wood, such as walnut, ½" (1.3cm) thick: 2 each 1" x 5" (2.5cm x 12.7cm)
- Paint, such as Miss Mustard Seed's Milk Paint: Luckett's green
- Finish: hemp oil, food-safe acrylic
- Sandpaper: assorted grits up to 400
- Pencil: white
- Graphite paper

TOOLS
- Band saw or scroll saw
- Carving knife, such as Flexcut KN12 detail knife
- #10 gouges: ⁹⁄₁₆" (14mm), such as Flexcut mallet tool; 1⅛" (29mm), such as Flexcut U-shaped carving gouge
- 70° V-tool: ¼" (6mm), such as Flexcut palm tool
- Spoon mule or vise
- Paintbrush: small

The author used these products for the project. Substitute your choice of brands, tools, and materials as desired.

Special Sources
For spoon mule plans by Elizabeth Sherman and Ryan Hardison, contact Elizabeth at liztnmaker@gmail.com.

GETTING STARTED

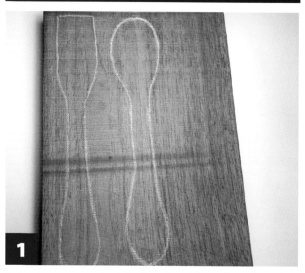

1

Select your wood of choice. For this project, I used kiln-dried walnut with fairly straight grain. Trace the pattern onto the wood. I used a white pencil, which was easier to see against the dark wood.

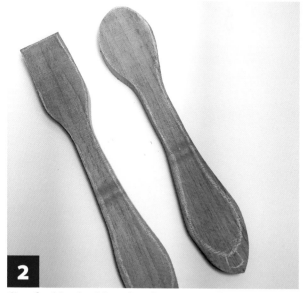

2

Cut the blanks. Use a band saw or scroll saw. Make sure the grain runs from the handle down to the bowl of the spoon or tines of the fork. Cut as closely as you can to the outline, leaving room around the top for the finial.

CARVING THE SPOON BOWL

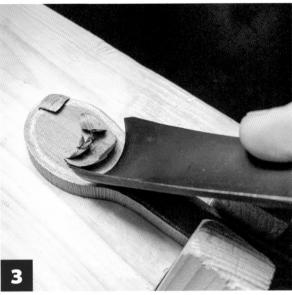

3

Carve the bowl of spoon. I used a ⁹⁄₁₆" (14mm) #10 gouge. Use a spoon mule or a vise to secure the blank.

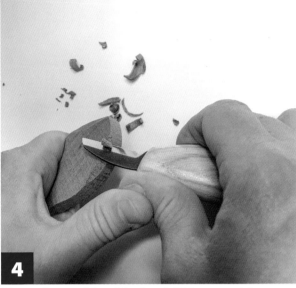

4

Shape the outside of the bowl. Using a straight carving knife, cut away excess from the bottom of the spoon bowl. For safety, always be sure to cut away from yourself.

CARVING THE FORK TINES

5

Trim the top of the fork blank. Keep the blank secured in the spoon mule or vise. Using a 1⅛" (29mm) #10 U-shaped gouge, thin it down to approximately half the thickness of the blank.

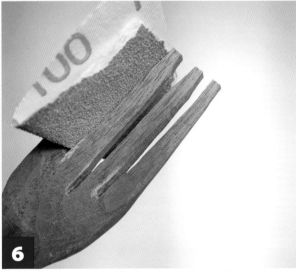

6

Cut the tines. Using the band saw or scroll saw, cut three vertical lines approximately 2" (5.1cm) long and spaced evenly apart. Gently sand in between each fork tine, shaping the ends as desired. Start with 100-grit sandpaper. Then move up progressively through the grits, smoothing out any rough spots or marks from the saw blade.

Caring for Your Utensils

Never place your handcarved utensils in
the dishwasher; always handwash. Do not
allow them to sit or soak in liquids. After
handwashing, pat them dry with a hand towel
or allow them to air dry. After some use, the
grain may feel rough. If this occurs, sand
lightly with 600-grit sandpaper and reapply
food-safe finish.

7

Shape the fork and spoon handles. Using the knife, begin making thin cuts down the side of the handle, removing the corners and shaping it as desired. Trim excess off the back of the blank. When carving the front of the blank, leave carved facets from around the middle to the end of the handle.

8

Carve the finial. Make both vertical and horizontal cuts to shape a small, decorative finial at the top of each handle.

9

Lightly hand-sand the inside and bottom of the spoon bowl. Depending on the smoothness of the cuts made, you can start with either 100- or 240-grit sandpaper. If the blank feels rough to the touch, you may need to start with 100-grit. If the blank feels fairly smooth to the touch, it may only need a light sanding or buffing with 240-, 320-, or even 400-grit sandpaper.

PAINTING AND DECORATING

10

Paint the handles. Using well-mixed milk paint, apply one light coat to both front and back of each handle. I used Miss Mustard Seed's Milk Paint in Luckett's green, a fresh, springy color. Allow to dry fully and then apply a second coat of paint. *Note: Make sure to only use paint on the parts of the utensils that won't be in direct, prolonged contact with food.*

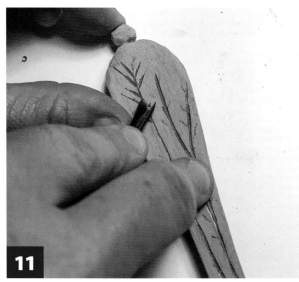

11

Lightly trace the leaf pattern onto the handles with graphite paper. You can also add your own freehand design, if you prefer. Carve the pattern into the wood using a ¼" (6mm) 70° V-tool. Brush the top of painted surface lightly with 400-grit sandpaper, applying quick, short strokes to remove any roughness from the carved pattern. This will also highlight the carved facets.

Finishing

Apply a food-safe wood finish to the spoon and fork. I used Miss Mustard Seed's Milk Paint food-safe hemp oil for the bowl and then applied a food-safe acrylic finish to seal in the paint. If time is not an issue, you can apply hemp oil directly to the painted handles and allow several days to two weeks for it to fully cure and seal in the paint.

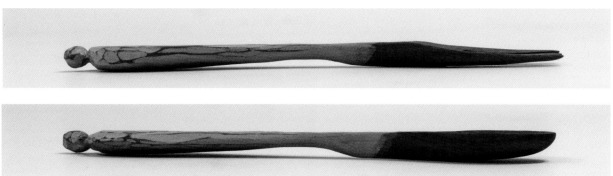

Swedish Courting Spoon

Dave Western

Pattern on page 88

Romantic wooden love tokens were popular throughout Europe from the mid-1600s to the early 1900s. This lovely little design is typical of the type of spoon a young man in Sweden might have given to a young woman he fancied. To increase his odds of a positive response, the young man might carve several of these spoons and give them to a variety of ladies, carefully observing how each was received. He could thus test the courtship waters without getting too involved!

Although spoons like these were technically quite simple and not overly adorned, they said a great deal about the young man's abilities, so they were made with great care. As for those receiving them, a particularly popular girl might accept spoons from several ardent suitors. She would often display them in a viewing rack for all to see, making her desirability clear to all who viewed them—and making it obvious who the best carvers were!

Utensils like this make wonderful, portable projects that can be undertaken with minimal space and equipment. In the old days, an axe, knife, and hook knife were likely the only tools used. Today, we can speed the process with drills, scroll saws, and sanders. I used power saws to make this spoon, but you can use any combination of tools you are comfortable with.

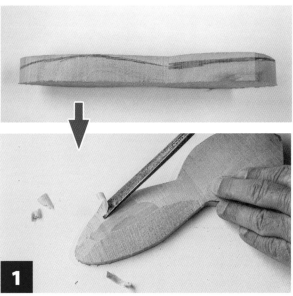

1

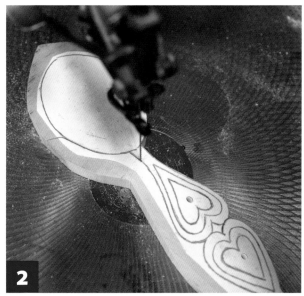

2

Prepare the blank. Use any light wood; I chose birch. Attach the pattern to the blank with repositionable spray adhesive and then cut the rough shape on a scroll saw, following the dotted line outside the perimeter of the pattern. Use an axe to lightly curve the back of the handle and bowl out toward the edges. Then use a ¾" (19mm) #1 chisel or straight gouge to further round the back of the handle. *Note: If you lack the tools, time, or patience to do this, you can simply make the spoon flat and straight.*

Drill the holes for the center sections. Then cut out the true perimeter and the interior hearts on the scroll saw. Alternatively, you can clear out these areas with a jeweler's saw or straight knife.

Materials & Tools

MATERIALS

- Birch, ¾" (1.9cm) thick: 2½" x 8" (6.4cm x 20.3cm)
- Spray adhesive: repositionable
- Pencils: graphite, colored
- Sandpaper: assorted grits up to 320
- Clean cotton cloths
- Finish: tung oil and beeswax polish

TOOLS

- Scroll saw with blades: #3 skip-tooth
- Axe
- Straight knife: 1" (25mm) blade
- #1 straight gouge or chisel: ¾" (19mm)
- #5 gouge: ⁹⁄₁₆" (14mm), or hook knife
- Drill with bits: small (optional)
- Needle files or scrapers
- Paintbrush

The author used these products for the project. Substitute your choice of brands, tools, and materials as desired.

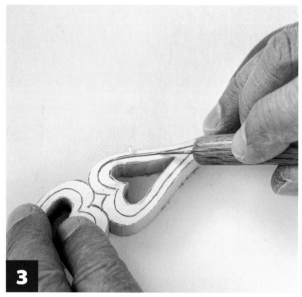

3

Add all the decorative lines on the handle. Use the knife and take shallow cuts.

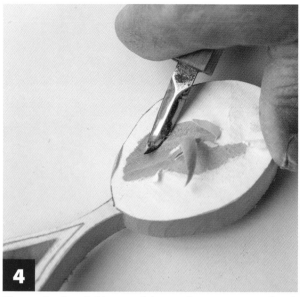

4

Shape the bowl. Use a ⁹⁄₁₆" (14mm) #5 gouge or a hook knife. I aim for a nice, fair bowl that is neither too deep nor too shallow. Once the bowl is shaped, sand it smooth, starting with 150-grit and then moving up progressively through the grits until you reach 320.

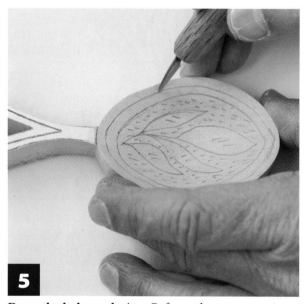

5

Draw the kolrose design. Refer to the pattern, using the straight knife to trace the design to a depth of just under ¹⁄₁₆" (0.2cm). Then, using the same tool, make a stop cut between the bowl and the handle and carve the handle down to it by about ¹⁄₁₆" (0.2cm). Use the knife or the ¾" (19mm) #1 gouge. This creates a visual separation between the parts of the spoon.

6

Shape the back of the bowl. Use the knife. I draw on colored pencil lines to keep the curvature even; dividing the lines over and over eventually results in a nice, even bowl shape. *Note: I use different colors to demarcate different levels. For added strength, I leave the handle as thick as possible where it connects to the bowl.* Clean up your cuts, deepening the designs on the bowl and handle where necessary.

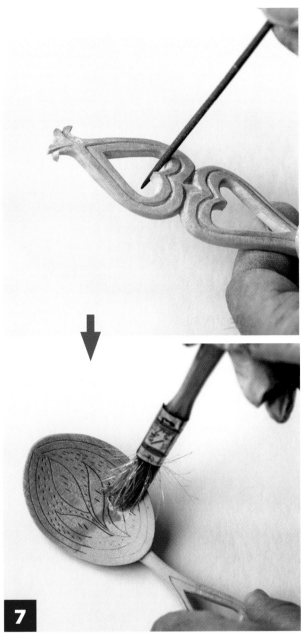

7

Sand and finish. Use sandpaper, files, and scrapers to smooth all carved facets. A needle file is excellent for smoothing interior curves. Then brush on a few coats of tung oil with an old paintbrush, removing the excess with a clean cotton cloth. Let dry for several days and then apply a coat of beeswax polish. Buff until you achieve a nice sheen and use or display as desired.

"Everything" Spoon

Karen Henderson

Pattern on page 89

I love the beauty of hardwood spoons for eating or serving. When I decided to carve a few, I realized I don't have the hand strength to use a hatchet to do most of the roughing out. Nor did I want to use power tools. So, my mentor, Frank Foltz, taught me to carve spoons from wet green wood. Using green wood, I can carve even hard fruitwoods, like apple, with knives and gouges. Frank has since left us, but his inspiration for beautiful spoons lives on.

Selecting the Wood

Many kinds of wood are suitable for carving spoons. Start with trees that have blossoms, such as apple, lilac, buckthorn, cherry, apricot, etc. Note that the wood needs to be green and wet; dried wood will not work for this technique.

Caring for Your Spoons

Handwash your spoons—do not put them in a dishwasher. If you let a spoon sit in liquid for an extended length of time, the grain may raise. If that happens, sand it with the finest grit of sandpaper possible and apply a thin coat of the finish.

ROUGHING OUT THE CARVING

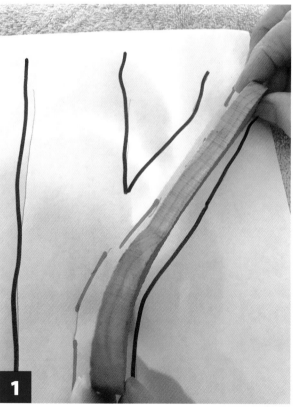

1

Plan the blank. Choose a portion of the tree that is at least 2½" to 3" (6.4cm to 7.6cm) in diameter with a branch to accommodate the handle. Cut the bowl of the spoon from the trunk of the tree. Do not use the center or heartwood; the grain in this section will always split.

2

Split the branch down the center. I use a band saw. Remove the rounded edge of the log and make the blank ½" (1.3cm) to ⅝" (1.6cm) thick. Transfer and cut the outline of the spoon. Adjust the outline to the natural shape of the wood; it doesn't need to be symmetrical.

Materials & Tools

MATERIALS

- Hardwood of choice cut into spoon shape (refer to pattern)
- Micro-finish sanding block
- Finish, such as Tried and True Danish Oil
- Abranet mesh sandpaper grits: 80, 120, 240, 320, 400, 500, 600 (some carving shops sell a sample pack so you don't have to purchase a roll of each grit)

TOOLS

- Band saw
- Carving knife
- #7 bent gouge: ¾" (19mm)

The author used these products for the project. Substitute your choice of brands, tools, and materials as desired.

TIP   FREEZING GREEN WOOD

Store green spoon blanks wrapped in a plastic bag in the freezer until you are ready to use them. This will keep them green and easy to carve.

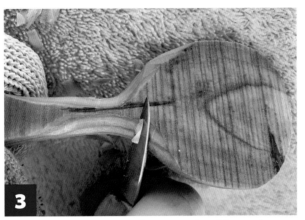

3 **Draw the keel line.** This line extends ½" (1.3cm) into the bowl and ½" (1.3cm) up the handle. This line helps you form the triangular keel, which strengthens the handle and supports the bowl. Carve the keel with the knife, and then blend it into the handle and bowl.

SHAPING THE CARVING

4 **Shape the back bowl of the spoon.** Work to create a gentle slope from the center of the bowl to the front tip and each side.

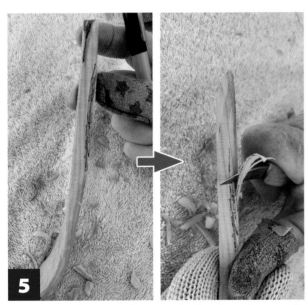

5 **Carve a gentle curve down to the bowl on the top of the handle.** Then thin it out from the back. Round the edges and check that it fits nicely into your hand. This will differ for right-handed and left-handed users.

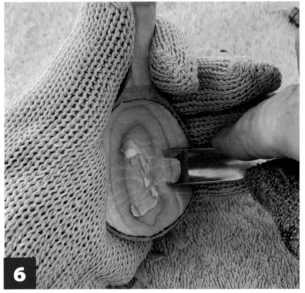

6 **Carve the bowl of the spoon.** Use a ¾" (19mm) #7 bent gouge. Start by carving across the grain. Work to create an even thickness throughout the bowl. Remember, an average eating spoon is only ⅜" (1cm) deep. Using your fingers to feel the thickness is usually the easiest. Once you're pleased with the thickness, carve with the grain to smooth the cuts. Carve to within ¹⁄₁₆" (0.2cm) of the edge.

7

Smooth the spoon. While it's possible to make clean cuts and use a scraper to finish the spoon, I use Abranet mesh sandpaper. It is more flexible and lasts longer than regular sandpaper. Start with 80-grit; I do 80 percent of my sanding with it. Use good lighting so you can work out any dips or bumps in the spoon. These will show when you apply the finish. Sand with the grain as much as possible. Then, sand with progressively finer grits of sandpaper: 120-, 240-, 320-, 400-, 500-, and 600-grit. A micro-finish sanding block helps; it has a hook and loop backing that works with the Abranet.

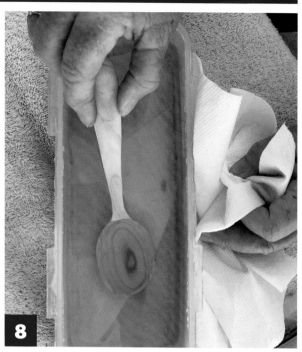

8

Apply a finish. I use Tried and True Danish Oil. Place the finish in a sealable container and lay the spoon in the oil. I let it soak for three days. Remove it from the oil and wipe off the excess. Let the spoon dry for three months, and it will not pick up flavor or color from the foods you are eating.

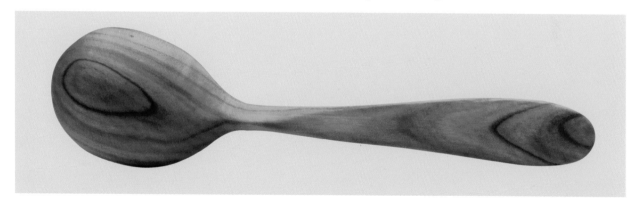

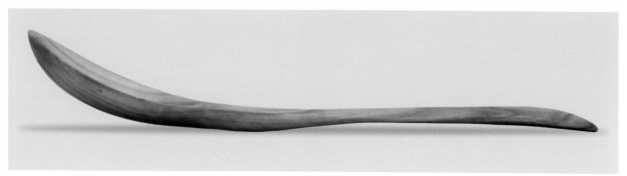

"EVERYTHING" SPOON

Whittled Jam Spreader

Chris Lubkemann

Most—if not all—of my carvings are done in green wood. That's just my style and you can easily find it when camping, hiking, or even in your backyard. For this project, choose a straight, knot-free branch.

Materials & Tools

MATERIALS
· Green branch, ¾" (1.9cm) in diameter: approximately 8" (20.3cm) long
· Fine-grit sandpaper
· Clear finish of choice (optional)

TOOLS
· Knife of choice

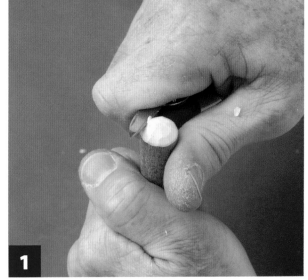

1

Prepare the blank. Choose your blank. I've chosen a little maple branch. Then round off the butt of the handle. Use the paring cut.

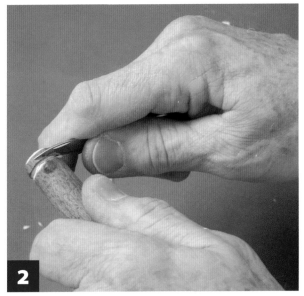

2

Cut grooves. Cut a little V-shaped groove around the end of the handle. Use the push cut. Then cut another groove farther down the handle. Locate this groove just a bit above where you want the blade of the spreader to start. Again, use the push cut.

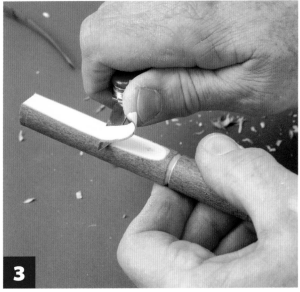

3

Flatten the blade of the spreader. Do this from both sides. Use long, straight strokes.

4

Shape the blade and neck. Continue carving until the blade is centered on the handle. Then narrow the neck of the spreader. Use both push cuts and paring cuts—always cutting toward the center—to narrow the part between the handle and the actual blade.

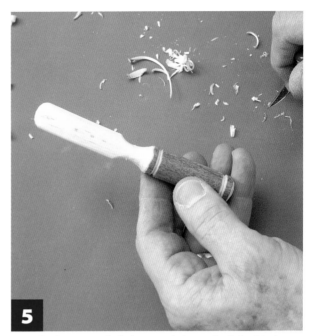

5

Finish shaping. Slightly round the end of the blade. Continue shaping the blade until you're satisfied.

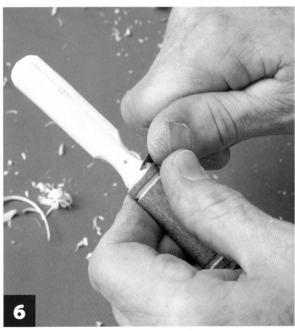

6

Finish the neck. Make another little V-cut groove between the neck and the handle.

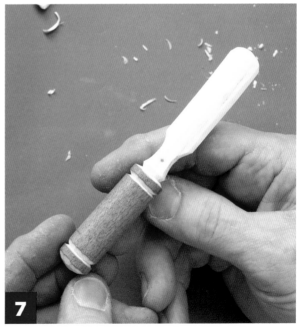

7

Add the final touches. Allow the spreader to dry a bit (if you used green wood). Then give it a final sanding. Apply a clear, food-safe finish of your choice (if desired).

PROJECTS
FOR BAKING

Volute Ladle

Mark Ivan Fortune

Pattern on page 89

A good friend once advised me that when choosing a fiddle, it's important to pay close attention to the volute. How that detail is executed will reveal the level of craftsmanship behind the entire instrument. Appreciating the beauty of the subject, I considered how I might incorporate the design into everyday objects, such as this ladle. Though my aim was not to match its level of refinement, I ventured to create an organic and elegant representation. Cedar is an excellent choice due to its natural antibacterial properties and, of course, for the delightful aroma it imparts.

Getting Started

Cut the blank on a band saw. It is important know that even with the best efforts, the templates may not align perfectly, and progress should be checked as the cuts advance, particularly in the area of the cylindrical head. Give some forethought as to how you'll hold the work during the carving stage. It is possible to secure the wood with a small clamp, using the waste from the band saw stage to cradle the spoon blank.

Materials & Tools

MATERIALS
- Wood, such as cedar, 1½" (3.8cm) thick: 3½" x 11" (8.8cm x 30cm)
- Pencil
- Sandpaper
- Small wooden splint
- Cabinet scraper
- Food-safe finish, such as raw linseed oil

TOOLS
- Band saw
- Spokeshave
- Pin for marking
- File
- #4 gouge: ⅜" (10mm)
- #5 gouges: ⅛" (3mm), 1½" (38mm)
- #6 gouges: ³⁄₁₆" (5mm), ½" (13mm)
- #9 gouge: ¼" (6mm)
- V-tool: ⅜" (10mm) 60°

The author used these products for the project. Substitute your choice of brands, tools, and materials as desired.

1 **Mark a rim around the edge of the spoon.** Using a 1½" (38mm) #5 gouge, carve the bowl. Work from the outside toward the center of the bowl. Aim for an even thickness.

2 **Flip the spoon over.** Mark a centerline down the length of the bowl. With a spokeshave, shape the back of the bowl, working each side of the centerline. Stay clear of the bowl edge as you concentrate your efforts on the high spots.

Hold the template against the side of the spoon. Make several pinholes penetrating through the paper and into the wood. Join the dots with a pencil. Repeat this on the other side, taking care to align the template for a well-formed, symmetrical design.

Begin to define the volute. With a ⅜" (10mm) 60° V-tool, cut around both faces of the volute, stopping on the first round of the spiral. The V-tool can be rotated to cut the walls of the volute at 90°. Be careful not to remove the pencil lines.

Establish the spiral. Using a ⅜" (10mm) #4 gouge, evenly blend the neck of the spoon into the volute's first spiral loop, down to the baseline. Complete steps 4 and 5 on both sides of the volute before moving on, continually checking for alignment.

Continue to define the spiral. Using a ½" (13mm) #6 gouge, round out the base of the curl. With the pencil, mark in the spiraling ramp as evenly as possible on both sides of the volute. With the ⅜" (10mm) 60° V-tool, carefully cut a track up the spiral on the waste side of the line.

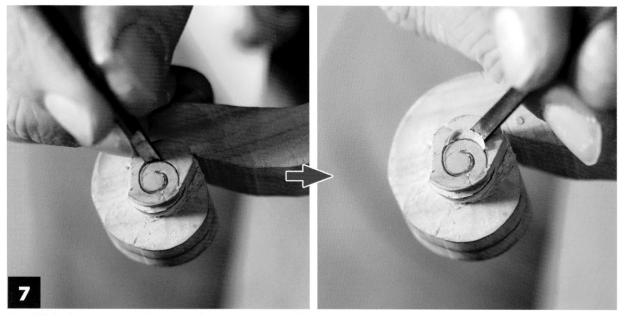

Establish the inner spiral. Use a ⅛" (3mm) #5 gouge for the tightest part of the inner swirl. Switch to a ³⁄₁₆" (5mm) #6 gouge as the curve widens. Carefully remove the waste.

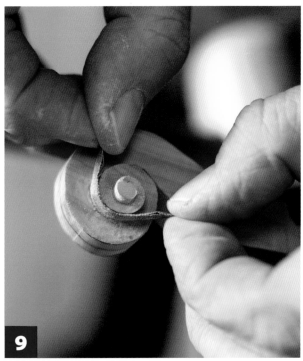

Carve the outer spiral. Use the ³⁄₁₆" (5mm) #6 gouge as you work your way down the spiral. Switch to the ½" (13mm) #6 gouge at the wider section.

Sand the volute. Use a narrow strip of sandpaper. Fold it lengthwise to sand the hard-to-reach curves and crevices of the volute. Be sure to check for alignment. Resist the temptation to further sand the spoon.

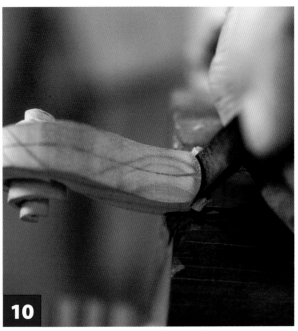

Flip the spoon over. Use a ½" (13mm) #6 gouge to create a stop cut under the base of the volute.

Use the pencil to mark a border around the base of the volute. Make two concave cuts along the back of the volute head using a ¼" (6mm) #9 gouge. It is imperative that the centerline where the two cuts converge remains centered and well defined.

12

Shape the front side of the volute head. Use the ¼" (6mm) #9 gouge. Be sure to protect the body of the spoon from the gouge by placing a small splint in the groove under the volute head.

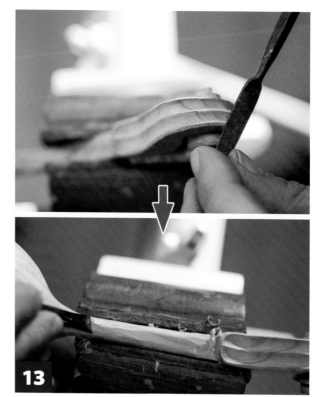

13

Round the edges. Use a file to chamfer the edges of the volute. With a flat gouge, round the edges of the back of the neck.

14

Clean up. Go over the spoon back with a cabinet scraper until your bowl is one homogenous form. Remove any remaining pencil or saw marks. Make finishing touches to the inside of the bowl with a gooseneck scraper.

Finishing

Wipe the spoon with food-safe raw linseed oil. The wood's natural cedar smell will soon return.

Stylized Sugar Spoon

Saskia De Jager

Pattern on page 90

I have always been drawn to functional art, as it adds beauty and pleasure to everyday tasks. I am fortunate enough to live in culturally rich Africa, which is home to more than 3,000 diverse tribes. This specific design was inspired by the jewelry of the nomadic Tuareg people who live across the Sahara Desert. These sugar scoops make great gifts and are fantastic conversation-starters.

Getting Started

Transfer the pattern to the blank, with the grain running down the length of the spoon. Use your preferred method; I used graphite paper and a pencil. Drill the blade-entry hole in the handle. Cut the inner part of the design using a scroll saw with a #5 skip-tooth blade. Then cut the perimeter.

Materials & Tools

MATERIALS
- Wood, such as kiaat, ⁹⁄₁₆" (1.4cm) thick: 1³⁄₁₆" x 3⁷⁄₁₆" (30cm x 87.5cm)
- Graphite paper
- Pencil
- Sandpaper: assorted grits up to 1000
- Finish, such as natural Danish oil
- Cotton cloths

TOOLS
- Scroll saw with blades: #5 skip-tooth
- Straight chisels: ³⁄₁₆" (5mm), ¼" (6mm)
- #3 gouge: ⁹⁄₁₆" (14mm)
- #10 gouge: ³⁄₈" (10mm)
- Drill with bit: small
- Paintbrushes

The author used these products for the project. Substitute your choice of brands, tools, and materials as desired.

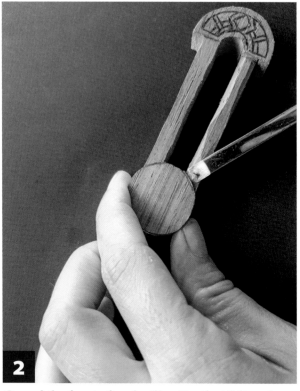

1

Rough out the spoon. Using a ³⁄₁₆" (5mm) and a ¼" (6mm) chisel, make stop cuts to separate the handle from the pillars and the pillars from the bowl. Then relieve the pillars slightly to create different levels on the carving.

2

Round the front of each pillar. Use the ¼" (6mm) chisel, making smooth cuts with the grain.

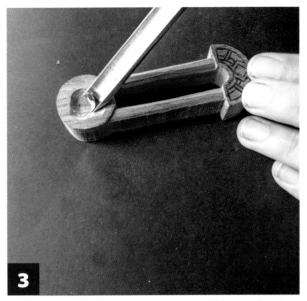

Carve the bowl of the spoon. Use a ⅜" (10mm) #10 gouge. You can make the spoon bowl as deep or as shallow as you wish; just be careful not to make it too thin, as it can break easily.

Carve the handle pattern. Follow the pattern lines with the ³⁄₁₆" (5mm) chisel, establishing small valleys between each section. *Note: You can use a V-tool or gouge of your choice for this portion; however, I prefer using a small chisel, which allows for finer detail.*

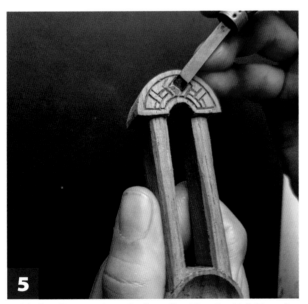

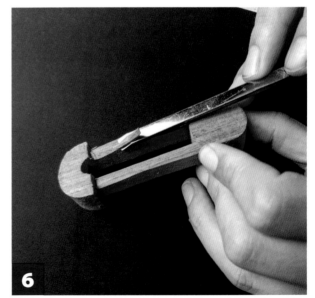

Add the diamond to the handle. Use the ³⁄₁₆" (5mm) chisel to make downward, sloping cuts toward the outside of the shape. Alternate between the four sides until you reach the desired depth and a sharp peak forms at the top.

Turn the spoon over. Round the backs of the pillars in the same way as you did the front. Use the ¼" (6mm) chisel.

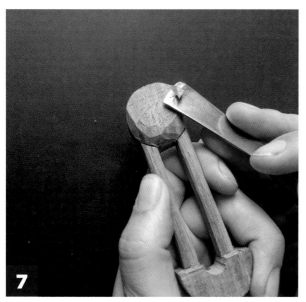

Round the back of the bowl. Use a ⁹⁄₁₆" (14mm) #3 gouge.

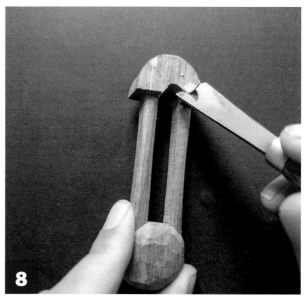

Thin the back of the handle slightly. Use the same tool, stopping just above the pillars.

Sand the entire spoon. Use 220-grit sandpaper, and then sand progressively through the grits until you reach 1000.

Finishing

Finish the project. Apply Danish oil over the entire surface using paintbrushes or a clean cotton cloth. Rub it in well and wipe off all excess. The number of coats you apply will depend on how glossy you want the scoop to be; I usually apply three coats for my desired look. I use Gobelins Original Danish oil, a South African brand, as a finish, because it is nontoxic and biodegradable. It also gives the wood a natural, matte look. I prefer a finish that provides permanent protection, as this lessens the need for periodic maintenance.

Fish Fin Measuring Spoon

Emilie Rigby

Pattern on page 90

My fish fin measuring spoon is a green woodworking project, meaning it should be carved out of wood that is fresh and uncured. The salmon design is a modified version of a whale tail scoop—a popular design in the green woodworking world. I have carved many whale tails over the years, but was inspired by an ichthyology class in college to modify the design with different fish tail forms. You can use it to scoop most things, from spices to loose leaf tea. When submerged, it is reminiscent of a tail fin kicking out of the water.

Getting Started

Prepare the blank. You can either transfer the pattern to a block of wood and cut it on a band saw, or take the unplugged route and rough it out with a hatchet. I've made a 1 Tbsp. (15mL) scoop for this tutorial, but feel free to alter it to whatever size you prefer. Trace the pattern on the blank. Feel free to leave a few extra inches on the handle past the tail. This will help you rough out the scoop more safely.

Materials & Tools

MATERIALS

- Green wood blank, such as cherry, alder, birch, or maple, approximately 2" (5.1cm) thick: 3" x 6" (7.6cm x 15.2cm)
- Oil pencils, such as Staedtler Black (a 6B pencil or charcoal from the campfire work, too)
- Sandpaper: assorted grits (optional)
- Food-safe finish, such as walnut oil

TOOLS

- Carving hatchet, such as Gransfors Bruks
- Handsaw, such as Silky BigBoy
- Carving knife
- Hook knife
- V-tool: ⅛" (3mm) 45°
- Small skew chisel, ⅛" (3mm) (optional)

The author used these products for the project. Substitute your choice of brands, tools, and materials as desired.

ROUGHING OUT

1

Make stop cuts just shy of your pencil lines on the neck of the scoop. Use a handsaw. I find it helpful to saw two parallel cuts on each side to avoid splitting the scoop bowl when you carve, due to the steep angles of the bowl and tail. Be sure that your saw is perpendicular to the blank; otherwise you risk splitting the neck of the scoop.

2

Rough out the back of the scoop with a hatchet.
Remove wood from the back of the scoop so the bowl
is rounded and the handle has a nice taper. At this
stage, it is important to only remove wood where you
feel confident and comfortable. Make sure there are
no hands, fingers, or legs in the path of your blade.
To improve accuracy, anchor your elbow on your hip
while cutting.

What Is Green Woodworking?

Green woodworking is the process of carving fresh,
uncured wood. It is easier to carve and often free
and fun to source. Instead of buying your materials
at the lumberyard, you simply need to make friends
with your local arborists and keep a good saw in
your car. Anyone who rides in the car with me
needs to be prepared to pull over so I can load
random logs into the car that someone put out by
the curb. This reduction in material cost can help
free you up to purchase higher-quality tools.

Some popular green woods to carve are cherry,
alder, birch, maple, walnut, and sycamore. I
recommend you avoid anything ring porous (such
as ash or red oak), anything too soft (such as pine
and cedar), or anything too hard (such as hickory).
I don't recommend using cured wood unless you
plan to carve this scoop with power tools and rasps.

3

Carve the profile of the spoon. With the hatchet,
carve toward your stop cuts, carving as close to the
pencil lines as you feel comfortable. Round the front
of the spoon. Now is a good time to saw off any extra
wood from the handle.

4

Carve the bowl with a hook knife. Grip the handle
of the tool in your fist, blade-side down, and carve
across the grain with shallow cuts until the scoop is
close to your desired thickness. Refer to the pattern.
Remember, any time you are carving toward yourself,
use your thumb as an anchor on the spoon to control
the path of the blade.

TIP | MEASURING SPOON VOLUME

Carvers have different approaches for achieving specific spoon volumes, but many of these are tedious, messy, and inaccurate. Some of what you're measuring with (oil, grain, water, etc.) always spills and requires a lot of cleanup and re-measuring. My favorite way to accurately gauge the size of scoops is to make a set of play dough measurements. Portion out the play dough to the popular measuring spoon sizes. Then you can easily test how big your scoop is. It's easy, clean, and reusable, and you can measure your scoop while you're carving it.

5

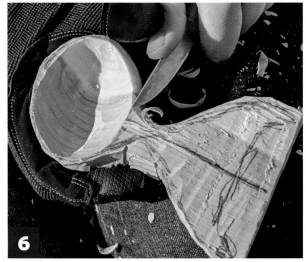

6

Round the outside of the bowl. Use the knife. For this part, small, shallow cuts work better and leave a nicer finish. Use a push cut for more control on the front of the bowl. Be sure to stop and inspect your project often to make sure you're carving both sides evenly.

Carve the neck of the scoop. For now, use the push cut only, carving inward from the widest to the thinnest point of the scoop on both sides. Uncontrolled knife cuts will result in the blade hitting into the grain of your scoop bowl. This will put micro cracks in your scoop bowl, which can in turn become macro cracks as the scoop dries.

ADDING THE DETAILS

7

Shape the back of the handle. I like to evenly slope the back of the scoop from the bowl to the end of the handle. Making small, shallow cuts, carve from the center to each edge, occasionally flicking the blade upward to create little curbs. Then carve the sloping end of the fin, removing a crescent-shaped slice (or series of slices) to create a point at each end.

8

Carve the base of the tail. Using a ⅛" (3mm) 45° V-tool, separate the tail from the bowl of the scoop. Use the knife to plane the fin down to the level of the deepest part of the cut you just made. You can also use a small skew chisel of your choice to round the base of the tail for a more realistic look. Then draw some guidelines with the pencil to indicate the direction of the fin lines.

9

Carve the fin lines. Position the ⅛" (3mm) 45° V-tool at the base of the tail and carve in a long, even line to the top of the fin. Carve several bigger outline cuts, and then fill in between them to make sure the lines fan out evenly from the base. Making sure your knife is extra sharp, make small, V-shaped cuts along the end of the fin to give the end of the handle a slightly jagged appearance. Sand or burnish the bowl as desired, but avoid sanding the fin section, as this can erase your fine detail work.

Finishing

Let the scoop dry. Green wood cracks (checks) if it dries at uneven rates. Since the wood fibers shrink as they cure, if one section is curing faster than another, it will pull itself apart and cracks will form. There are two main ways to avoid this: Make sure the bowl thickness of your scoop is consistent, and slow down the drying process. Scoops with very even bowl thicknesses can just be set on a shelf in your home for a few days. If you have a lot of mass on the front of your scoop, I encourage you to put it in an open zip-top bag. This will create a more humid environment, so it dries slowly. Another option is to bury it in green woodchips to even out and slow the drying.

Once the spoon has dried for several days, coat it in a food-safe oil. I prefer walnut oil because it is a drying oil and has a pleasantly mild aroma. However, if you plan to gift the piece to someone with nut allergies, choose an alternative, such as linseed, coconut (solid at room temperature), canola, or an oil-and-beeswax mixture for extra waterproofing. Try to avoid oils that go rancid, such as olive oil. Allow time for the spoon to absorb the oil and dry. Then it's ready to use! Handwash only and re-oil any time the finish starts to get dull.

Rustic Coffee Scoop

Josh Rittenhouse

Pattern on page 90

The spoon remains a fun challenge for even the most experienced carvers, adding to its lure and appeal. And it's so much more than just the hollowed-out end of a stick. Spoon carving is about tradition, design, shapes, form, and function. In this type of woodworking, you learn about edge tools and body mechanics—all while sampling a variety of local woods that might otherwise never make it to your workbench. As is the case in much of woodworking, the handcarved spoon occupies a different sphere than its mass-produced substitute. And, in my opinion, coffee spoons are the most fun to make.

Getting Started

Ideally, spoon carving is a green woodworking craft. You can experiment with a great range of local woods, usually for free. Fruitwood, while dense, can provide unique, attractive blanks. Avoid using porous wood like oak or ash, as it's harder to carve. Ultimately, when it comes to wood type, just try whatever you have access to. Make sure to start with a round big enough to split in half and exclude the pith from the wood you intend to use.

Materials & Tools

MATERIALS
- Greenwood, such as cherry, approximately 2" (5.1cm) thick: 3" x 5½" (7.6cm x 14cm)
- Pencil
- Food-safe finish, such as beeswax and walnut oil

TOOLS
- Small handsaw, such as a bow saw
- Carving axe
- Scorp or hook knife
- Carving knife

ROUGHING OUT

1

Split the round with an axe. Once it's scaled down to a usable size, be sure to cut off any knots or other defects.

2

Prepare the blank. Using a carving axe, begin to flatten the faces of the wood and work the sides parallel to each other. It's not crucial to make a perfect rectangle, but getting something close will make it easier to hold.

Establish the crank. *Note: The crank is the angle of the bowl in relation to the handle.* I work from the handle side first, axing down toward the lowest point of the angle. Then I work from the tip of the bowl toward the handle to form a V—this establishes the crank. Don't worry about the deep V, as you'll round it out later.

Draw the outline of the scoop onto the blank. I freehand mine, but you can use a template if desired. *Note: Use pencils darker than the standard #2, as they show up better on green wood.*

Rough out the shape. Use the axe. I tend to shape the outline of the scoop first. Next, I move on to the side profile.

Trim the sides. Using the axe, make stop cuts in from the sides toward the base of the handle. It's important to cut the fibers against the grain before cutting down the handle toward the bowl. If you drive your axe too far in while cutting down toward the bowl of the scoop, you'll end up with a crack in that area later.

Define the shape. Use a knife with a large blade, such as a Mora. I work from the widest point toward the tip of the bowl first, and then go in the opposite direction. Working from the widest point of the bowl in both directions will help avoid getting under the grain and tearing out sections you don't want removed.

ADDING THE DETAILS

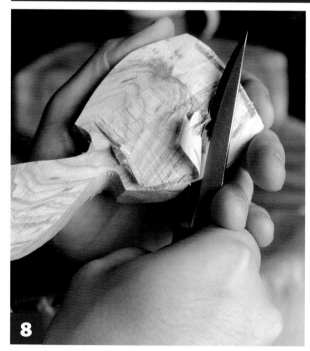

Round and clean up the edges. Move from the bowl to the handle. Before you move on to hollow the bowl of the scoop, redraw the shape to refine your curves.

Hollow the bowl. Using a scorp or hook knife, start at the tip of the scoop and work toward the handle first.

Remove the waste. Cut across the grain to remove rows of chips at once, and begin to shape the bottom part of the bowl.

Add the finishing touches. Finishing cuts should be thin and delicate and provide a smooth, shiny surface. With the carving knife, refine your cuts to establish just a few smooth, flat planes across the surface. Add small chamfers to the edges to remove any sharp corners.

Apply a food-safe finish. I use a 2:1 mix of beeswax and walnut oil that I make myself. Butcher-block finishes also work well. Be sure to apply a liberal amount. Give the finish time to cure, and you'll be ready to start using your new scoop!

PROJECTS
FOR SERVING

Walnut Soup Scoop

Kevin Kaminski

Pattern on page 91

This scoop is a superb item for serving your favorite soup or chili. Walnut is a great hardwood to work with—not too hard, yet durable enough to get years and years of use. For some of my spoons, I've had to alter the shape of the rim to avoid a flaw in the raw wood block, but I've found that people admire the unique shape. I've designed this scoop with just such a deviation from a regular oval bowl, giving it an interesting profile and increased artistic appeal.

Materials & Tools

MATERIALS

- Walnut, 3½" (8.9cm) square: 12½" (31.8cm) long
- Spray adhesive
- Sandpaper: assorted grits up to 220
- Mineral oil: food-grade

TOOLS

- Band saw
- Vise
- #8 bent gouge, such as Pfeil: 1" (25mm)
- Knife: rough out (optional)
- Microplane (snap-in handle) with blades: 8" (20.3cm) coarse flat, 8" (20.3cm) coarse rounded
- Shop-made sanding blocks: flat with felt surface, rounded with felt or other soft surface
- Bar clamps

The author used these products for the project. Substitute your choice of brands, tools, and materials as desired.

Getting Started

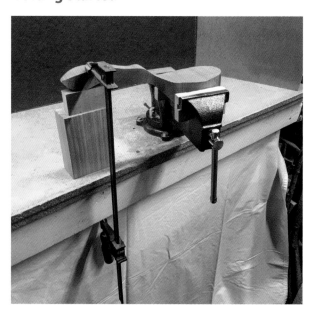

Select a block of wood with as few defects as possible. "Interesting" grain is fine but can lead to challenges. Transfer the template onto the blank with spray adhesive, making sure the grain travels vertically up the handle. Cut out your blank on a band saw and secure the area where the bowl of the scoop will go in a vise. Then secure the handle area to your bench with a bar clamp.

ROUGHING OUT

1

Begin carving inside the bowl of the scoop. Draw the inside wall of the scoop about ¼" (0.6cm) inside the outer edge. Using a 1" (25mm) #8 sweep bent gouge, start at the line and begin carving in toward the center of the scoop.

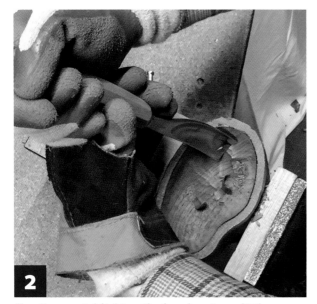

2

Continue establishing the bowl, going a little deeper each time. Use the same tool. Remember that at this stage, you want the wall of the scoop to go straight down. As you dig down deeper, stop periodically to ensure that the walls are still fairly vertical and make corrections as needed. Once you've nearly reached the bottom, start sloping the front and back into the center of the bottom of the bowl, trying to maintain a consistent ¼" (0.6cm) to ⅜" (1cm) wall thickness as much as possible. Use many lighter strokes to carve out the transition from the vertical to the curved bottom.

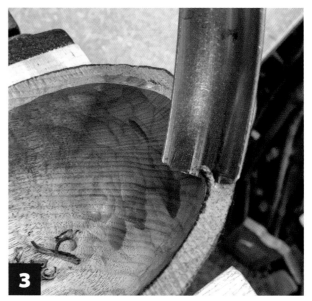

4

Sand the inside of the bowl. Drag a quarter sheet of sandpaper (I fold it in thirds lengthwise) along the surface with one hand. Maintain control by applying pressure with the thumb or fingers of the other hand.

3

Trim the sharp corner on the inside of the bowl. Use the spoon gouge so you won't have to sand too much to round over the edge later.

SHAPING AND FINISHING

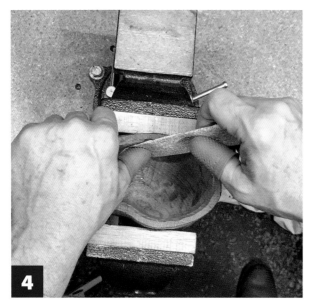

5

Refine the inside of the bowl. Move progressively up through the grits, from 80 to 220, until you are satisfied that each grit has removed the sanding marks of the previous one.

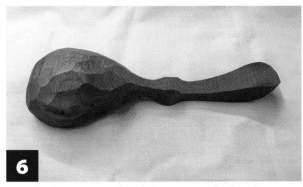

6 Cut the basic outer bowl shape. Use the band saw or a rough out knife. Remove large portions of the block around the bottom of the bowl of the scoop.

7 Shape the outside of the rim. Mount the handle of the scoop in the bench vise. Using sandpaper—or microplanes, as long as you use a light touch—sand the top and outside rim. Then smooth the connection to the handle.

8 Shape the outside of the bowl. Turn the scoop upside down in the vise. Then use a stick that reaches to the ground with a soft cushion (such as a cloth) placed inside the bowl; this will support the scoop and prevent scratching as you work the outside areas. Shape the outside of the bowl of the scoop with the microplanes. Use the flat blade for the convex surfaces (most of the outside of the bowl) and the rounded ones for the concave surfaces, smoothing the bowl into the handle. Check the thickness of the walls and bottom of the scoop for consistency as you shape the outside. Make adjustments to the thickness of the walls as necessary.

9 Sand the outside of the bowl. Use a flat sanding block. Then switch to a rounded sanding block to smooth the areas sweeping into the handle; I used a dowel with sandpaper wrapped around it.

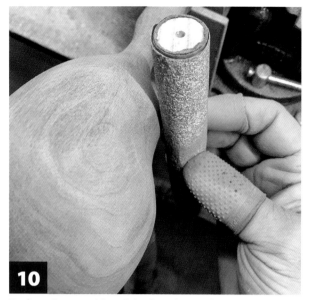

10

Refine the outside of the bowl. Use the rounded sanding block. Sand up through the grits until you reach 220. Keep sanding until the outside of the bowl is smooth and to your liking.

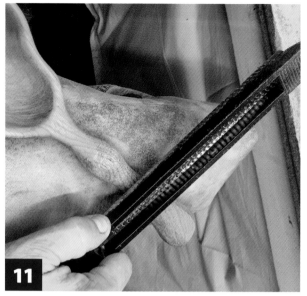

11

Shape the handle. Holding the scoop with one hand, use the two microplanes to bring the corners to a more rounded shape.

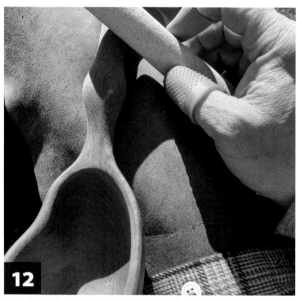

12

Sand the handle. Use shop-made sanding blocks or dowels to sand the handle up through the grits until you reach 220 and are happy with the shape. The goal is to smooth the handle surface so it flows seamlessly into the bowl.

13

Apply a food-grade mineral oil. Rub it thoroughly into the surface of the scoop. At least three applications will suffice; make sure to let it air dry on a rack for several hours in between applications.

TIP **PROTECT YOUR FINGERS**

Carving with gloves for protection is very tiring on the muscles of the hand. Use Rubber Finger Tips for great control and less damage to the pads of your fingers. I use Tory Red Cap Fingertips and Swingline Rubber Finger Tips, available in different sizes.

WALNUT SOUP SCOOP

Cherry Leaf Bowl

Brian Bailey

Pattern on page 91

This small wooden bowl can be used as a candy dish, as a catchall for keys and change, or as a standalone decorative piece. The bowl is easy to carve and makes a great gift or sale item.

I carve my bowls from scrap lumber that I can't use in my furniture-making business, so the cost of the wood is negligible. Any scrap board with an attractive grain will work. If you'd prefer not to use the included pattern, just devise your own, letting your imagination and the figure of the wood be your guide.

Materials & Tools

MATERIALS

- Cherry or wood of choice, 1" (2.5cm) thick: 6½" x 12" (16.5cm x 30.5cm)
- Sandpaper: 120- to 220-grit
- 0000 steel wool
- Minwax antique oil
- Johnson's paste wax
- Soft cloth for buffing

TOOLS

- #2 gouge: ½" (13mm)
- #5 gouges: ⅜" (10mm) long bent, ½" (13mm), ⅝" (16mm)
- #7 gouge: ⅜" (10mm) long bent
- #9 gouge: ½" (13mm)
- #11 gouge: 3⁄16" (5mm)
- Scrapers: card and curved

The author used these products for the project. Substitute your choice of brands, tools, and materials as desired.

ROUGHING OUT

1

Cut the blank. Use the figure of the board as a guide to draw in a cherry leaf. Cut the leaf to shape using a band saw. Draw a line approximately ⅜" (1cm) in from the top edge to establish the bowl cavity and the inside edge of the lip.

2

Draw in the major landmarks. Draw a line on the bottom, 1" (2.5cm) in from the edge, to establish the bottom of the bowl. Then draw a line around the outside edge approximately ¼" (0.6cm) down from the top to establish the bottom of the lip.

Shape the tip of the leaf. Clamp the blank to the bench and begin to taper the tip area with a mallet and a ⅝" (16mm) #5 gouge. The tip tapers and twists downward from the main plane of the bowl. By carving in the tip shape first, you can easily blend the outside bowl profile into the tip.

Carve the outside profile. Clamp the blank edgewise in a vise. Use the ⅝" (16mm) #5 gouge and the guidelines to carve a concave profile between the lip and the bowl bottom. You may need to clamp the bowl face down on the bench for some cuts.

5

Rough out the bowl cavity. Use extra-strength double-sided carpet tape to secure the bowl to your vise or work surface. Hog out the waste wood in the bowl cavity with a ½" (13mm) #9 gouge. Stay inside your guidelines, creating gently sloped walls. Keep the bowl bottom about ⁵⁄₁₆" (0.8cm) thick at this stage.

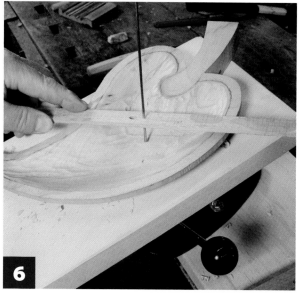

6

Check the depth of your bowl. I use a homemade depth gauge to make sure I don't carve the bottom of the bowl too deep. If you substitute a pencil for the metal rod shown here, the pencil will leave marks on the wood. Keep carving the wood away until the depth gauge stops leaving a pencil mark.

SMOOTHING AND SHAPING

7

Smooth the sides and bottom of the bowl. I use several gouges that fit the profile of the area I'm carving. For this project, I used a ½" (13mm) #2 and a ½" (13mm) #5 gouge. I switched to a ³⁄₈" (10mm) #5 and a ³⁄₈" (10mm) #7 bent gouge for some of the tight curves.

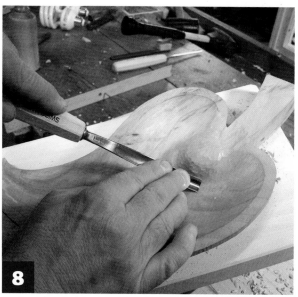

8

Refine the bottom of the bowl. Use the ³⁄₈" (10mm) #7 gouge to smooth the transition between the walls and the bottom of the bowl. Use the same gouge to begin shaping the stem knob that protrudes into the bowl cavity.

9

Finish shaping the bowl. I used a card scraper and a curved scraper to shape the lip and to smooth the sides and bottom of the bowl. Work to produce a smooth flowing surface on the inside of the bowl. You do not need to smooth the outside of the bowl.

10

Begin shaping the top of the stem. Use your gouges of choice to carve a gently curved stem. Do not carve the stem straight out from the bowl. Taper the sides of the stem for a rounded look and blend the stem into the stem knob.

11

Shape the bottom of the stem. Remove the bowl from the vise and peel off the carpet tape. Clamp the bowl face down on the bench and shape the bottom of the stem with the ½" (13mm) #2 gouge. Use a ³⁄₁₆" (5mm) #11 gouge to blend the stem into the sides.

12

Shape the end of the stem. Clamp the bowl edgewise in a vise and shape the end of the stem. I used the ⅜" (10mm) #7 gouge to recess and notch the end of the stem for a decorative look.

13

Refine the bowl. Inspect the bowl from various angles, looking for areas that can be improved. On this bowl, the stem knob was too large, so I used a scraper to make it smaller.

14

Smooth the inside of the bowl. Use scrapers, and then sand with 120-, 150-, and 220-grit sandpaper. Use the same process to smooth the stem. Strive for a smooth, flowing look and feel.

15

Add texture to the outside of the bowl. Carve random facets around the outside of the bowl with the ⅝" (16mm) #5 gouge. Pencil in a line ¼" (0.6cm) from the edge of the bowl and recess the bottom of the bowl about 1/16" (0.2cm) deep with the ⅝" (16mm) #5 gouge. Sand away any sharp edges with 220-grit sandpaper.

16

Finish the bowl. Sign your name and date on the bottom of the bowl with a woodburner. Apply two coats of Minwax antique oil. After the oil dries, rub on a coat of Johnson's paste wax with 0000 steel wool. Let the wax glaze over and then buff it out with a soft cloth.

CHERRY LEAF BOWL

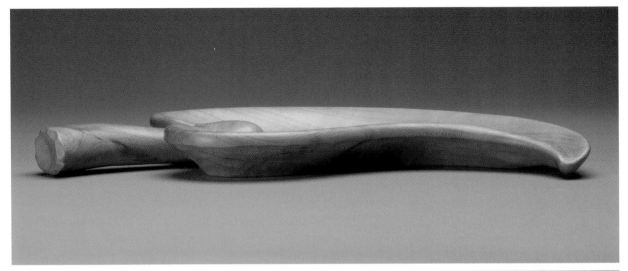

Turned and Carved Bread Bowl

Luke Voytas

Pattern on page 92

A few years ago, I started carving and painting some of my turned bowls to add color to craft show displays and to avoid my most dreaded task: sanding. Many of my bowls now feature a carved outside, which is then coated in food-safe milk paint and sanded back to provide contrast and reveal the grain of the wood. Although I primarily use this technique for functional bowls, you can apply it to all sorts of carving. Whether you make functional work or decorative and whimsical carvings, milk paint is a versatile and forgiving medium. It's also a good way to add interest to woods that may otherwise be a bit bland.

Choosing Wood for Bowls

The white ash I used for this bowl doesn't offer a lot in terms of figure and color, but with some carving and paint, it becomes quite eye-catching. You can use any wood, but denser hardwoods, such as maple, cherry, walnut, or ash, are best. They turn well and also carve nicely. I turn my wood green—when the wood is fresh-cut and has a high moisture content—and carve the bowl fresh off the lathe, when the wood is easiest to work with. It's important to keep green, turned bowls thin, with walls less than ½" (1.3cm) thick, and consistent from rim to base. I've also chosen a shape that will allow me to carve easily from the base to the rim. You can scale this shape up or down depending on how the piece will function.

Keep in mind that bowls with a decorative foot at the base prevent the gouge from accessing the very bottom of the bowl. Forms with outflowing curves are also more difficult to carve, as you must hold the tool at a difficult angle in order to make successful cuts.

Materials & Tools

MATERIALS
- Hardwood, such as ash, cherry, or walnut, 3½" (8.9cm) thick: approximately 9" x 10" (22.9cm x 25.4cm)
- Sandpaper, such as Abranet: assorted grits up to 400
- Scotch-Brite pads: coarse
- Sandpaper: 320-grit
- Disposable cup
- Popsicle stick
- Paint, such as Real Milk Paint Co.: deep sapphire
- Finish, such as food-safe linseed oil
- Old towel
- Cotton cloths
- Scrap wood

TOOLS
- Lathe with bowl gouge
- #9 gouge: ½" (13mm)
- Sander: orbital
- Clamps
- Brush: natural bristle

The author used these products for the project. Substitute your choice of brands, tools, and materials as desired.

ROUGHING OUT

1

Turn the bowl on the lathe. Mount the blank using a faceplate or woodworm, and then shape the outside using a bowl gouge. Create a form that will be easy to carve, either with a continuous or gentle curve.

2

Remount the bowl to the lathe using a four-jaw chuck. Turn the inside, being careful to keep the walls at an even thickness, around ⅜" (1cm). Then sand the bowl using 120-grit Abranet sandpaper, moving up progressively through the grits until you reach 400. The fine mesh of this sandpaper doesn't clog up when sanding green wood and efficiently removes any tear-out and tool marks.

4

Carve around the rest of the base. Use the same tool. Then move down through the remainder of the bowl. Try varying long and short strokes to create a consistent but somewhat random pattern. You can also rotate the bowl as you work, completing a series of "rings" around the bowl to create a tiered effect. Stop around 1" (2.5cm) before the rim on all sides.

3

Place the bowl upside down on a workbench. It should sit at a height that allows you to get your body above the workpiece in order to drive the gouge through the wood. Place an old towel or cloth under the bowl to prevent marring, and place a piece of scrap wood under that in case the gouge slips. You can clamp the bowl to the bench if needed. Begin carving the bowl, starting at the base (right where the outer walls start). Use a ½" (13mm) #9 gouge or one of your choice. Hold the tool at a steep angle to the surface and drive downward with your dominant hand, using your non-dominant hand for control. As you move down, also pull up and out of the cut. This keeps each cut short and controlled. If desired, use a mallet to drive the gouge down; this can help to keep the cuts from wandering.

5

Carve the final strokes up to the rim. At this point in the project, slow down and work more carefully. Use short, controlled cuts; you can always remove material, but you can't put it back! Don't cut into the actual rim. Pull the gouge up and out of the cut at the end of each stroke for a clean chip. Inspect the piece and make any final tweaks.

6

7

Mix up the paint. I'm a big fan of Real Milk Paint Co. products, and for this project, I chose their deep sapphire color. Mix the powdered paint in a disposable cup with a craft stick. You're looking for a smooth consistency, similar to a thin milkshake, free of lumps. A thinner mixture will create more of a wash. You can always apply multiple coats if you want the color to appear more opaque. You could also layer one color one over another for a unique effect.

Paint the exterior of the bowl, leaving the bottom untouched. Use a natural bristle brush. While you paint, work in the same direction in which you carved, or the paint will build up on the ridges of the carving. Let the paint dry.

8

9

Lightly sand the outside of the bowl. Use an orbital sander with 320-grit sandpaper. The goal is to cut through the paint at the highest points on the carved surface to reveal the depth and texture of the carving. You can also use fine sandpaper or a Scotch-Brite pad, if preferred. Gently wipe off the excess dust with a cotton cloth.

Smooth the base of the bowl slightly. Use the orbital sander. Then apply a finish of your choice; as I intend my pieces to be used for food consumption, I use a food-safe polymerizing linseed oil made by Tried and True finishes. Let dry. Once the oil has fully cured, the bowl is ready for use!

TURNED AND CARVED BREAD BOWL

Hardwood Salad Servers

Brad Tremblay

Pattern on page 92

I made these simple salad servers in an afternoon, and with some determination, you could easily shape your own in time for dinner! Perfect for indoor or outdoor entertaining, the set effortlessly elevates any dish. *Note: Always wear a carving glove and thumb guard. These photos were taken without them to clearly show hand and knife positions.*

Materials & Tools

MATERIALS
- 2 greenwood blanks, 1" (2.5cm) thick: approximately 3¼" x 11" (8.2cm x 28cm)
- 4B pencil
- Burnisher
- Food-safe finish, such as mineral oil

TOOLS
- Crosscut handsaw
- Axe
- Sloyd knife, such as Mora 106
- Hook knife, such as Mora 164
- Coping saw or scroll saw

The author used these products for the project. Substitute your choice of brands, tools, and materials as desired.

PREPPING AND CARVING

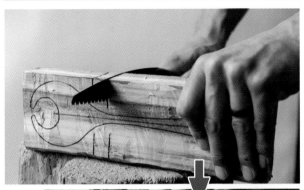

1

Transfer the patterns to the blanks. A soft pencil, such as a 4B, works best on greenwood. Using a crosscut handsaw, make two parallel stop cuts on each side of the neck of the bowl. Do this on both blanks. Then cut the profiles with an axe.

2

Define the profile. Using a sloyd knife, start at the widest part of the handle and make long, slicing cuts toward the neck. Do the same on the opposite side. Check for symmetry and adjust if needed. Do this for both spoons.

3

Blend the neck, making sure to work with the grain.
Do this for both spoons. If you find you are lifting or tearing off pieces, you're likely going against the grain. Strive for long, deliberate cuts. *Note: The thumb-pull technique is ideal for the tip of the bowl—since it's all cross-grain there, it will require a little more force. Place the handle of the knife in your hand, resting it on the inside of your second knuckle. Roll your fingertips over the handle to hold it without closing your hand completely. Extend your thumb, place it on the edge of the bowl, and close your fist, pulling the knife blade through the cut. Offset your thumb to the side to avoid injury.*

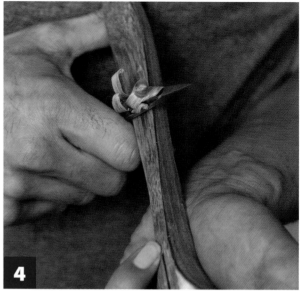

4

Shape the top profile. Using the pencil, mark lines for the goal thickness along the entire side of your spoon. Work your knife around the profile, using the line as a reference and making controlled cuts around the rim. Repeat this process on the bottom of the handle until you've achieved the desired thickness. Do this for both spoons.

5

Shape the back of the bowl. Use the thumb-push technique to carve with the grain. Place the blade directly in front of your thumb and push the back of the blade forward. Your non-carving thumb is doing most of the work here; your carving hand is there for support. Turn the spoon around and use the same method to carve from the middle of the spoon to the neck. Start in the center of the bowl to define the curve, and then work your way forward and out to the sides. Do this for both spoons.

6

Cut the tines. Use a coping saw or a scroll saw.

7

Define the bowl. Draw a line around the inside of the bowl approximately ⅛" (0.3cm) in from the edge. Cutting across the grain, use the hook knife to carve out the bowl, starting at the center. Continue carving the inside edges of the bowl as you slowly work your way toward the line. Do this for both spoons.

9

Burnish and oil the set. Using a hard piece of seasoned wood or a burnisher, rub the entire spoon to compress the fibers and polish it. Apply a liberal amount of a food-safe mineral oil to the entire piece and let it dry overnight. Use multiple coats for maximum saturation.

FINISHING

8

Soften the edges. Blend the bowl rim into the top of the handle. Refine the inside cuts of the tines. Chamfer and round all sharp edges that remain. Do this for both spoons.

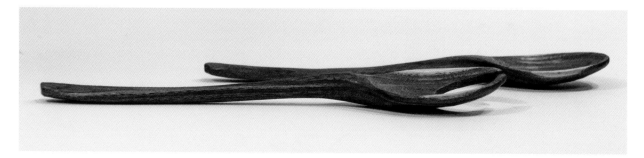

Whimsey Spoon

Shirley Adler

Pattern on page 93

This spoon was adapted from an old Welsh design. You can make the chain as long as your wood allows; just continue to trace the links until you get the number you want.

Getting Started

Transfer the pattern to the wood. Cut the front view. Transfer the side view to the wood. I trace the pattern on tissue paper and glue the tissue paper to the side. Then cut the side view. Remove wood from the front and back of the handle to keep the design centered. Sketch the transition from the bowl to the handle.

Materials & Tools

MATERIALS
- Wood, 1½" (3.8cm) thick: 3½" x 11" (8.9cm x 27.9cm)
- Sandpaper
- Oil finish
- Rags for finish

TOOLS
- Knife
- Gouge of choice (I use a #5 spoon)
- Micro gouge

The author used these products for the project. Substitute your choice of brands, tools, and materials as desired.

CARVING THE CHAIN

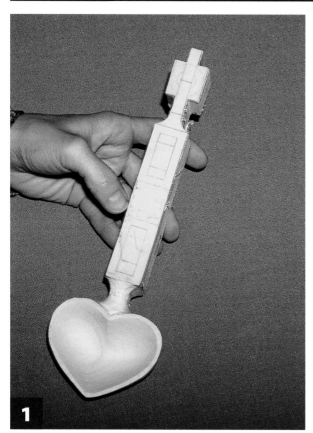

1

Carve the inside of the spoon bowl. Use a spoon gouge. Use a knife to carve the outside of the bowl. Use your fingers to check for imperfections in the bowl wall. Draw the lines for the ball and the cage on all four sides of the blank.

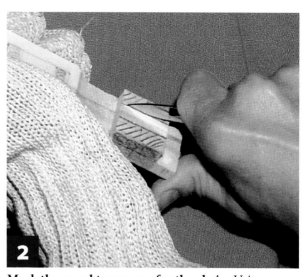

2

Mark the wood to remove for the chain. Using a knife, make a stop cut on the line perpendicular to the surface of the wood. Then, use a slicing cut to remove the material up to the stop cut.

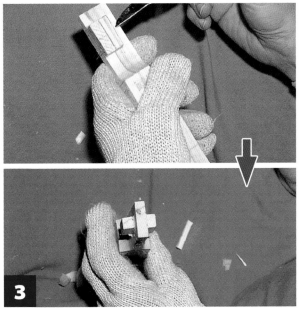

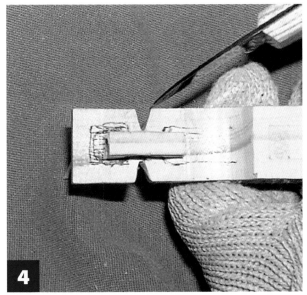

3

Repeat the stop cuts and slicing cuts. Shape the chain section until it resembles a cross from the end.

4

Carve V-shaped grooves between the links. Use the knife. This starts to separate the two links. Use a pencil to shade the material to remove from inside the links.

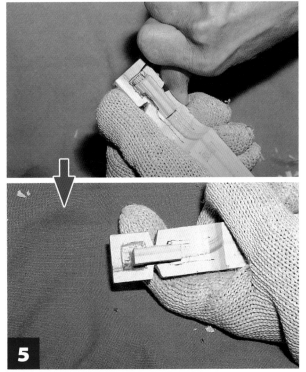

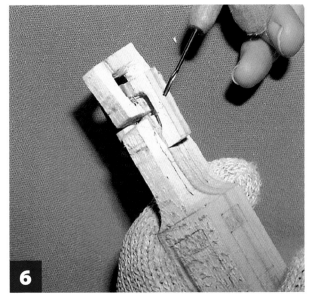

5

Make stop cuts along the interior lines. Carefully slice up to the stop cuts to remove the wood from inside the links. Repeat the process to remove as much wood as possible from inside the links.

6

Remove the remaining wood holding the links together. Use a micro gouge and the knife. Once the link is free, round and smooth it with the knife. Repeat steps 4–6 to complete the rest of the links.

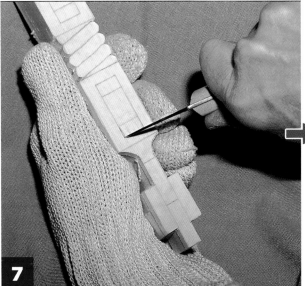

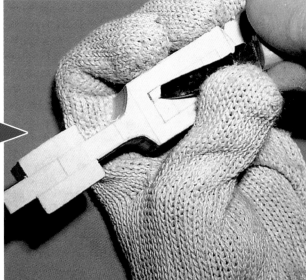

7

Make stop cuts around the open area above and below the ball. Use the knife. Make these cuts perpendicular to the surface of the blank to keep the cage bars even and straight. Slice up to the stop cut to remove the wood around the ball, but do not carve any wood from the ball yet.

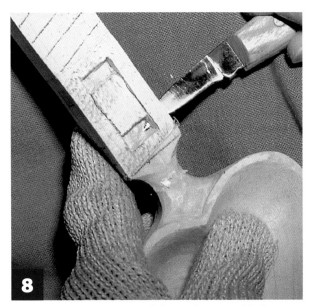

8

Continue removing wood from above and below the ball. As you repeat the stop and slicing cuts, the knife blade will eventually show through.

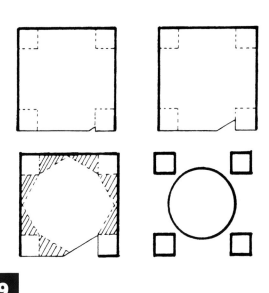

9

Visualize the ball within the cage. This illustration shows the ball and cage from the end. Plan a series of stop and slicing cuts that will free the ball from the bars of each cage.

WHIMSEY SPOON

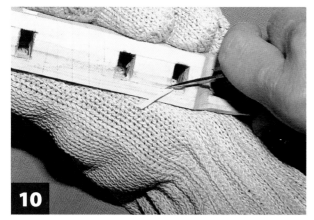

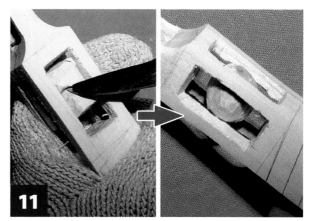

Make a stop cut along the bar on top of the ball. The cut must be perpendicular to the surface of the wood. Use the knife. Carefully slice up to the stop cut to begin shaping the ball. As you carve, round the ball. It is easier to round the ball while it is still captive.

Continue rounding the ball. Eventually, you will cut the ball free from the cage. Once it is free, move it around in the cage as you continue rounding it. The goal is for the ball to roll freely in the cage. Repeat the process for the second ball-in-cage.

CARVING THE SPIRAL

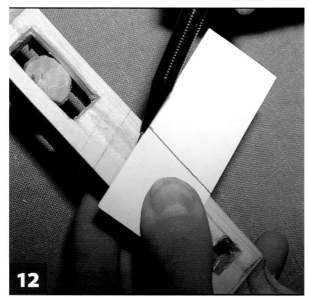

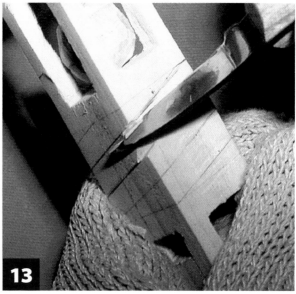

Mark the spiral on all four sides of the handle. Place the straight edge of a strip of cardstock along the spiral line on the front of the handle. Mark the points where the vertical edge of the handle meets the card. Draw a line to connect those points. Rotate the spoon 90° and align the line on the cardstock with the edge of the handle. Position the top edge of the cardstock where the spiral line ended on the previous face and use the cardstock to continue the spiral around all four sides.

Make stop cuts along the spiral pattern lines. Use a slicing cut to round and smooth the spiral to the stop cuts around the handle.

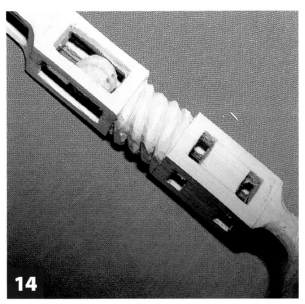

14

Round the spiral section. Use the knife to remove most of the material on the corners to make the entire spiral section round. Smooth any rough areas on the spoon.

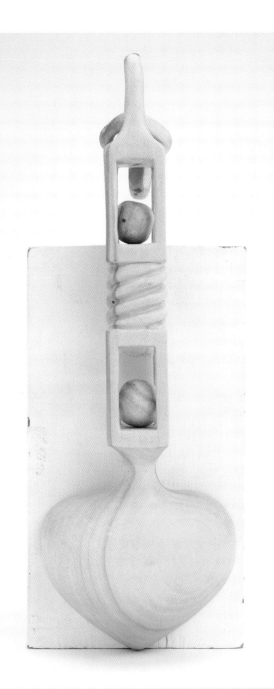

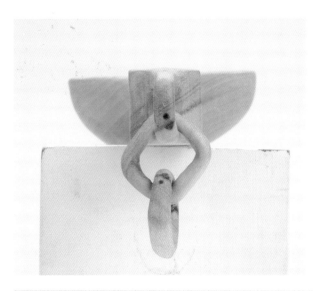

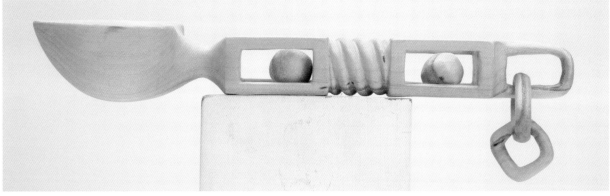

Bushcraft Spoon

Jon Mac

Pattern on page 93

When I started carving thirteen years ago, I decided to limit my tools to just three: axe, knife, and hook knife. These tools are simple to maintain and extremely useful at camp. I'm a keen hiker, so I can easily carry these tools and something to sharpen them on a camping trip and produce some folk art.

However, some time ago, I wondered if it was possible to carve a good-quality spoon without using a hook knife. After some experimentation, I managed to produce a spoon that was tidy and yet unusual in its bowl shape.

Getting Started

I generally carve green birch or sycamore. However, most green wood can be carved into a spoon, so choose a variety that's available to you. Choose a branch that is clean and free of knots or other branches.

I use a sharp axe with a slim profile at the cutting edge. I used a Gransfors Bruk large carving axe for this tutorial, but I also use handmade axes from Nic Westermann. You can also rough out the spoon with a knife, but it will take longer. The general roughing-out procedure is the same regardless of the tool.

Materials & Tools

MATERIALS
- Green log, 3" (7.6cm) in diameter; 8" (20.3cm) long
- Tung oil

TOOLS
- Axe
- Knife

The author used these products for the project. Substitute your choice of brands, tools, and materials as desired.

Special Sources
Gransfors Bruk's large carving axe is available from Greenwood Direct, *greenwood-direct.co.uk*, or Highland Woodworking, *highlandwoodworking.com*.

For more on Nic Westermann's hand-forged edge tools, visit *nicwestermann.co.uk*.

ROUGHING OUT THE PROJECT

Split the log in half. Use the axe. Then split one of the halves into quarters. Split a rectangular piece from one of the quarters. Remove all of the sapwood and bark. Shape the wood into a 1" by 2" by 8" (2.5cm by 5.1cm by 20.3cm) blank.

Draw the outline of the spoon onto the blank. Feather some cuts into the side of the blank, cutting toward the bowl at around a 25° angle. Make each subsequent cut above the first and close to the previous cut. These cuts form the sweep from the handle into the bowl.

First set of feather cuts

Second single cut

Chop from the other side at a 50° angle to remove the triangle of waste wood. Repeat steps 2 and 3 on the other side of the bowl. Work to create some symmetry so the bowl meets the handle at the same place on both sides.

3

4

Add a curve to the bowl. Make feather-like cuts with the axe from a point just above the bowl to the center of the bowl.

5

Turn the spoon so the bowl faces you. Hold the axe head in your hand and carefully remove the waste wood. This is a tricky moment, so take your time. Stop when your spoon looks like the second photo.

Remove the point from the back of the handle. Create a flat surface curving nicely from the bowl/handle transition to the end of the handle.

Remove the waste from the back of the handles and upper half of the bowl. Chop two large chamfers down each side of the spoon from the middle of the bowl through the end of the handle. You can see the large triangles of wood I removed in the second photo.

8

Remove the waste wood from the lower half of the spoon. Use the techniques explained in steps 6 and 7. You should now have something resembling a spoon.

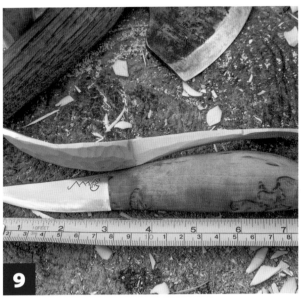

9

Round and shape the spoon. Use a knife. Tidy up the shape of the outside of the bowl before you start to carve the inside.

CARVING THE BOWL

10

Draw a centerline on the top of the bowl. Then, add two offshoots from near the center to the front corners of the bowl. Push the point of the knife into the intersection of these bowl guidelines and rock the blade down along the line. Repeat for the other two lines to make the three initial stop cuts. Don't worry if the knife doesn't reach the whole way to the bowl edge; this is simply your starting point.

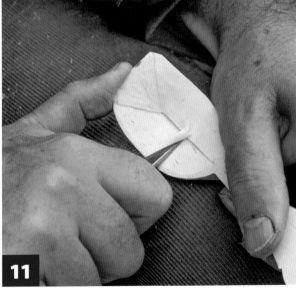

11

Carve up to the cuts. Make shallow sliding cuts up to the stop cuts to hollow the bowl. Deepen and elongate the cuts as needed.

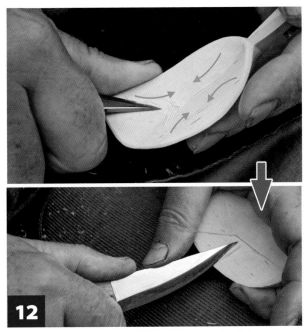

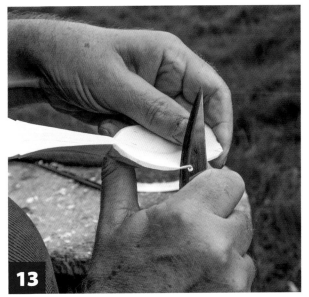

13

Chamfer the edge of the spoon bowl. Run the knife carefully around the outside edge at a 45° angle. Clean up the carving, and go around the spoon until everything is symmetrical where needed.

12

Carve the spoon bowl. Move around; don't favor one side or area. Be careful because you will encounter a strip on each side of the bowl face where the grain runs into the center. Use the tip of the knife to gently smooth the intersection where the grain changes direction. Be precise and remove very thin slivers, using your thumb as a fulcrum for control.

FINISHING THE PROJECT

14

Decorate the spoon if desired. Add a little kolrosing or chip carving to the handle. Then, apply a coat of oil finish; I prefer tung oil.

Patterns

SIMPLE POCKET SPOON

photocopy at 125%

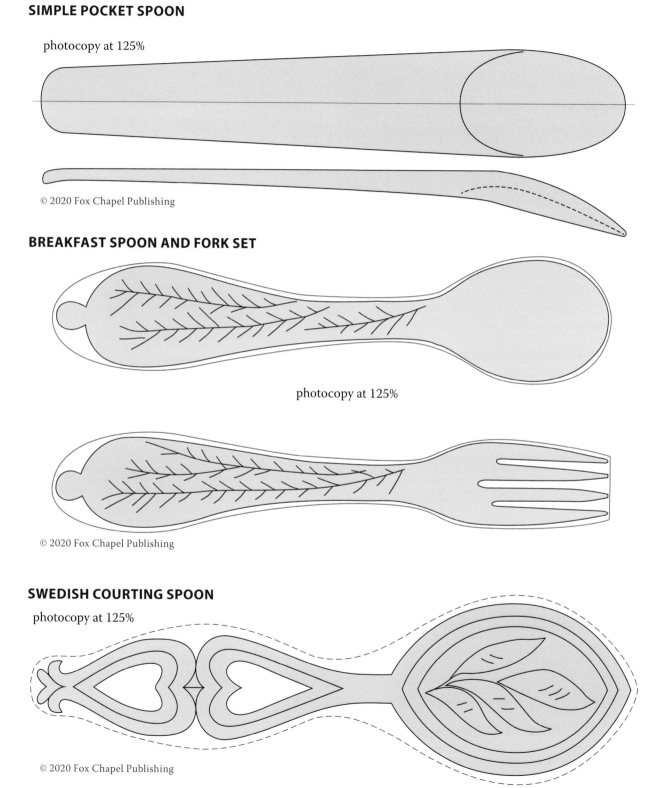

© 2020 Fox Chapel Publishing

BREAKFAST SPOON AND FORK SET

photocopy at 125%

© 2020 Fox Chapel Publishing

SWEDISH COURTING SPOON

photocopy at 125%

© 2020 Fox Chapel Publishing

"EVERYTHING" SPOON

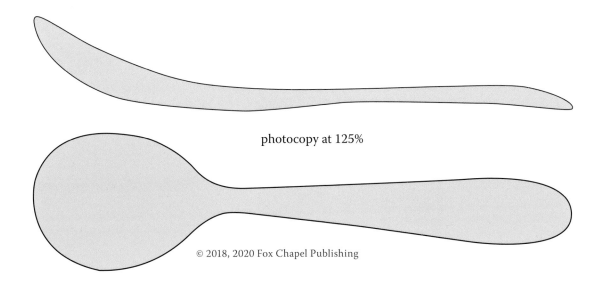

photocopy at 125%

© 2018, 2020 Fox Chapel Publishing

VOLUTE LADLE

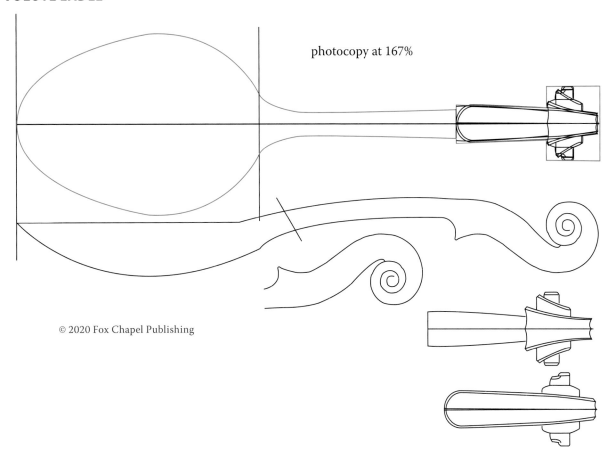

photocopy at 167%

© 2020 Fox Chapel Publishing

STYLIZED SUGAR SPOON

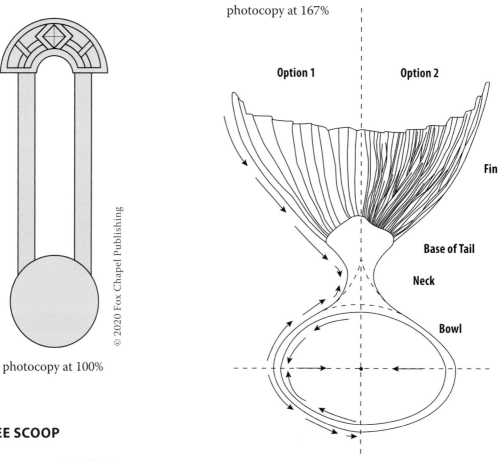

photocopy at 100%

© 2020 Fox Chapel Publishing

FISH FIN MEASURING SPOON

photocopy at 167%

Option 1   Option 2

Fin

Base of Tail

Neck

Bowl

© 2020 Fox Chapel Publishing

RUSTIC COFFEE SCOOP

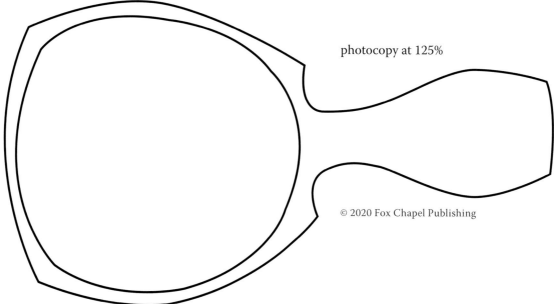

photocopy at 125%

© 2020 Fox Chapel Publishing

WALNUT SOUP SCOOP

photocopy at 200%

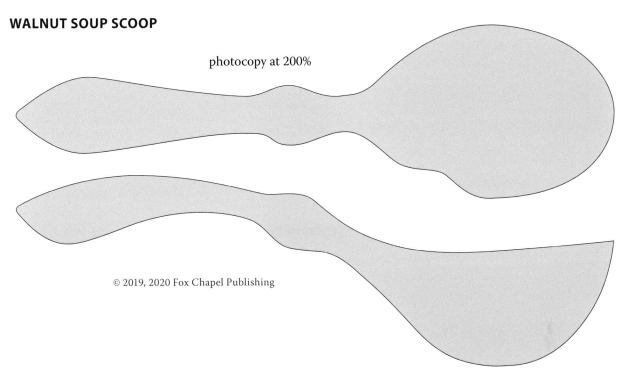

© 2019, 2020 Fox Chapel Publishing

CHERRY LEAF BOWL

photocopy at 200%

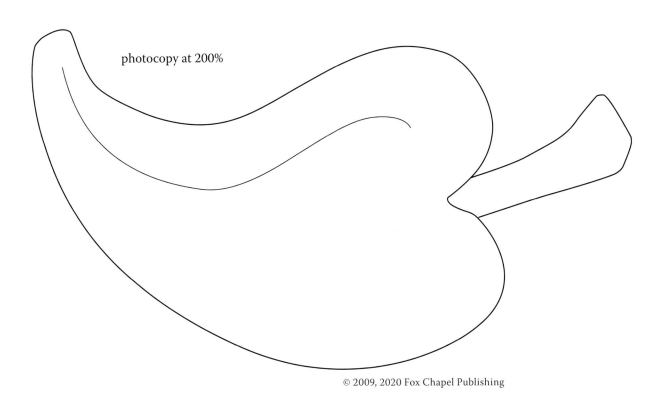

© 2009, 2020 Fox Chapel Publishing

TURNED AND CARVED BREAD BOWL (PROFILE)

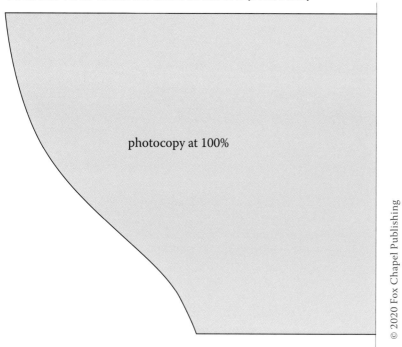

photocopy at 100%

© 2020 Fox Chapel Publishing

HARDWOOD SALAD SERVERS

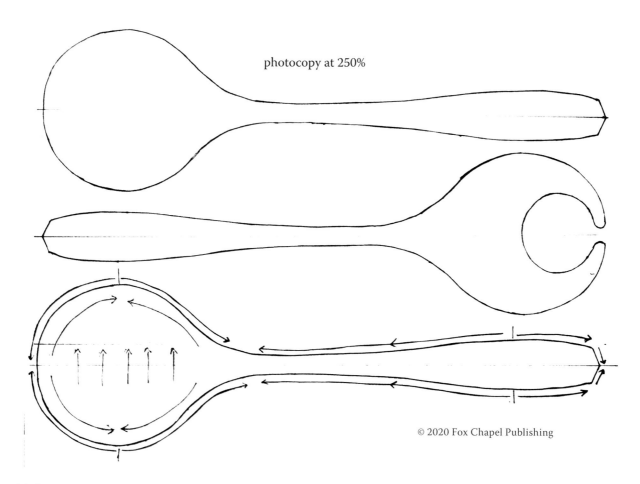

photocopy at 250%

© 2020 Fox Chapel Publishing

WHIMSEY SPOON

BUSHCRAFT SPOON

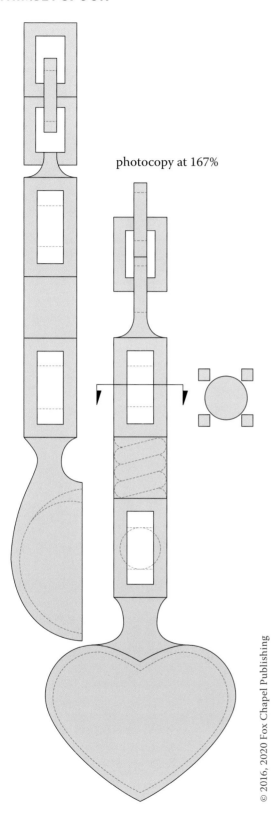

photocopy at 167%

© 2016, 2020 Fox Chapel Publishing

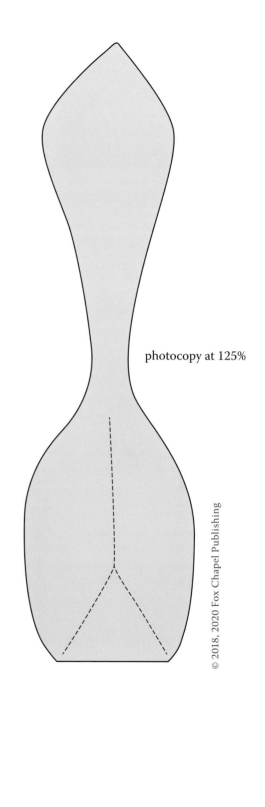

photocopy at 125%

© 2018, 2020 Fox Chapel Publishing

About the Authors

Emmet Van Driesche is a professional spoon carver, writer, and farmer living in western Massachusetts. He publishes *Spoonesaurus Magazine*, a print-only publication that celebrates the craft of spoon carving. Find out more about him at *EmmetVanDriesche.com* or follow along on Instagram at @emmet_van_driesche.

Elizabeth Sherman, an artist from Tennessee, began carving approximately two years ago as a hobby. She is a self-taught carver and enjoys creating handcrafted functional art, such as spoons and other handcarved pieces. She frequently can be found at local markets and fairs with her two children, and, on occasion, they can also be seen carving wooden spoons with her. Elizabeth teaches spoon carving classes and hosts spoon gatherings in the southeastern United States. Contact her on Instagram and Facebook at @liztnmaker or email her at liztnmaker@gmail.com.

Dave Western is a professional lovespoon carver and the author of two books on carved lovespoons, both available from *foxchapelpublishing.com*. Dave carves on commission and also teaches classes. For more of Dave's work, visit *davidwesternlovespoons.com*.

Karen Henderson is retired. She began carving in 1998 and enjoys a variety of types of carving, such as caricatures, bark, and especially spoons. She teaches carving and enjoys sharing her ideas with other woodcarvers at a weekly gathering of carvers during the winter. Karen lives in St. Francis, Minnesota.

Chris Lubkemann has been carving since age 7. *The Little Book of Whittling* is his second book with Fox Chapel Publishing. His first was *Whittling Twigs and Branches*. The project included in this book was his second to be featured in *Woodcarving Illustrated*. His first, "Whittling a Miniature Flower," appeared in Holiday 2004 (Issue 29).

Mark Ivan Fortune followed a traditional apprenticeship in stone carving to become a Master of his craft with more than twenty years of experience. Since 2008, he has turned his attentions primarily to woodcarving. He teaches from his home workshop at Raheenwood in East Clare, Ireland. Contact him at markivanfortune@icloud.com.

Saskia De Jager started selling her carvings under the brand Ash & Elm in 2015, after she and her partner moved to a small Karoo town in South Africa. Regardless of the growing culture of machine-carved wood, Saskia believes in preserving the art of handcarving. She has created hundreds of handcarved wooden pieces of art, which are sold all around the globe. Find her on Instagram at @ash_and_elm.

Emilie Rigby is a green woodworker living in a little cabin on a lake in Upstate New York. She spends her time sitting by the lake carving spoons, writing stories, and illustrating the natural world. She can be found on Instagram at @emiliesrigby or her website *emilierigby.com*.

Brian Bailey retired after working for the state of New York for almost thirty years. For the past twenty-five years, he has been sawing and drying his own lumber. He started carving as a youngster and has been carving off and on since then.

Jon believes that the skills of using and maintaining knife and axe blades need to be shared so that we do not lose these important techniques. For more of his work, visit *spooncarvingfirststeps.com*.

Shirley Adler is a spoon carving instructor from Denver, Colorado.

Josh Rittenhouse has been involved with woodworking his whole life. At a young age, Josh could always be found in his father's woodshop helping out with various projects. He began carving spoons in 2015 and has carved hundreds since. Find Josh on Instagram at @ partakegoods and online at *partakegoods. com*.

Luke Voytas is the Wood Shop Technician and Artist Instructor at the GoggleWorks Center for the Arts in Reading, Pennsylvania. Learn about and sign up for his classes at *GoggleWorks.org*. Find more of his work at *LukeVoytas.com*.

Brad Tremblay lives in southern Ontario with his wife and two dogs. He has been carving spoons for two years. Brad discovered his love for spooncarving through bushcraft and backcountry camping trips. Find him on Etsy at TheSpoonStudio.

Kevin Kaminski has been carving spoons and other treenware since 2005. He especially enjoys working in local hardwoods that are durable and sustainable. He lives in New Castle, Delaware. Contact him at wizardstower1@gmail.com.

Jon Mac and his wife, Sarah, live in southwest England, near Dartmoor National Park. Jon carves kuksa, ale hens, and spoons, and he is working on chip carving. He is a keen hillwalker, has served with the local mountain rescue team, and teaches team building and survival skills. A knife designer, Jon works closely with Chris Grant, one of the British Isles' foremost knife makers.

Index

Note: Page numbers in *italics* indicate projects and patterns. Page numbers in **bold** indicate author bios.